Advance praise for *Creative Int*

M000078528

"Organizations will not be in the phone book five to seven years from now unless they understand the significance of creativity and creative leadership. Rowe's useful and readable book provides rich insights about how creativity affects the bottom line."

—Warren Bennis
Distinguished Professor and co-author of *Geeks and Geezers*,
Harvard Press

"In *Creative Intelligence*, Alan Rowe makes a compelling case that creativity is essential for success in today's complex, rapidly changing world, and that all of us can discover and unlock our creative potential. He presents a clear and practical roadmap for how we can understand, measure, and apply our creative capabilities. Moreover, Rowe shows how leaders can develop creative talent and support creativity throughout their organizations. This book is a must read for anyone seeking creative solutions to life's difficult and messy problems."

—Tom Cummings
University of Southern California School of Management

"*Creative Intelligence* convinces you that you do possess creativity. It shows you how to determine the types you have, and encourages you to do something with your talents."

—Gerald Nadler
IBM Chair Emeritus in Engineering Management, University of
Southern California, and co-author of the bestseller *Breakthrough*
Thinking

"Like passion, creativity is highly prized in people and companies, yet so difficult to manufacture. *Creative Intelligence* shows how both people and companies can harness creativity as a competitive advantage to get to their goals."

—Louis Columbus
Sr. Analyst, AMR Research

"Alan Rowe makes an important contribution to our understanding of human creativity in the most comprehensive book yet written on this subject. He offers a powerful new instrument for measuring creative intelligence and provides penetrating and provocative insights on how education can be reformed to produce more creative individuals, and how organizations can position themselves to tap the creative potential of all their employees."

—Dr. Burt Nanus
Co-author, with Warren Bennis, of *Leaders: Strategies for Taking Charge*; **author of** *Strategies for Taking Charge, Visionary Leadership,* **and** *Leaders Who Make a Difference*

"This book is an extraordinary effort that will challenge people to become 'all that they can be.' Most people can make significant contributions if they recognize their potential. Our society is changing rapidly and creative approaches to education are needed to maintain our competitive position in the world."

—Dr. Robert R. Dockson
Former CEO and Chairman, CalFed, Inc.

"After a very successful career in industry and education, Alan Rowe has provided us with a roadmap to understanding creativity. His examples clearly show how we can enhance our lives and make the world a better place in which to live. He has produced an important work that is highly readable and extremely useful. He demonstrates how we can all learn how to use our creative ability to assure human progress. This is a book that I would recommend to business executives, educators, organization leaders and anyone interested in enhancing their own lives."

—Stephen Bollenbach
CEO, Hilton Corporation

CREATIVE INTELLIGENCE

INTELLIGENCE

Discovering the Innovative Potential
in Ourselves and Others

Alan J. Rowe

PEARSON
Prentice
Hall

An Imprint of PEARSON EDUCATION
Upper Saddle River, NJ • New York • San Francisco • Toronto • Sydney
Tokyo • Singapore • Hong Kong • Cape Town • Madrid
Paris • Milan • Munich • Amsterdam

www.informit.com/ph

Library of Congress Cataloging-in-Publication Data

A CIP catalog record for this book can be obtained from the Library of Congress

Editorial/Production Supervision: Wil Mara
Cover Design Director: Jerry Votta
Cover Design: Anthony Gemmellaro
Art Director: Gail Cocker-Bogusz
Buyer: Maura Zaldivar
VP, Editor-in-Chief: Tim Moore
Editorial Assistant: Richard Winkler
Marketing Manager: John Pierce

© 2004 Pearson Education, Inc.
Publishing as Prentice Hall
Upper Saddle River, New Jersey 07458

Prentice Hall PTR offers excellent discounts on this book when ordered in quantity for bulk purchases or special sales. For more information, please contact: U.S. Corporate and Government Sales, 1-800-382-3419, corpsales@pearsontechgroup.com. For sales outside of the U.S., please contact: International Sales, 1-317-581-3793, or via the Web at international@pearsontechgroup.com.

Printed in the United States of America

This product is printed digitally on demand.

ISBN 0-13-815792-8

Pearson Education Ltd.
Pearson Education Australia Pty., Limited
Pearson Education Singapore, Pte. Ltd.
Pearson Education North Asia Ltd.
Pearson Education Canada, Ltd.
Pearson Educación de Mexico, S.A. de C.V.
Pearson Education—Japan
Pearson Education Malaysia, Pte. Ltd.

TABLE OF CONTENTS

PREFACE

Creativity that is not used is wasted.

Finding Your Creativity

We all follow different paths as we go through life. Which is the right one? How do we choose? These are questions with which we are all confronted. For example, have you ever wondered how you compare with Edison, Shakespeare, or Churchill? We take for granted that they were creative, but are you also creative? **A basic premise of this book is that "everyone" has creative potential and that anyone can "discover his or her hidden creative potential."** Often, we are not aware of our potential or the environment does not encourage our being different.

Is there a straightforward way for you to determine whether you are creative? One way is to review the lives of famous people, such as Galileo, who have clearly demonstrated their creative ability. What were they like? What did they have in common? What price did they pay in order to be creative? These and similar questions will be examined by studying a number of well-known individuals to determine which underlying factors or conditions helped them to be creative.

Another important consideration is can we determine what "drives" some people to "go beyond" the ordinary? The evidence shows that certain personalities have the drive to achieve outstanding results. This appears to be true regardless of the field in which the person works. The perspective here is that we can determine Creative Intelligence using a test instrument that will be described in Chapter 2. We define Creative Intelligence as a combination of the personality we have, how our mind processes information, what are our personal values, and does the environmental support our efforts? These factors form the foundation that will be used to explore creativity and to show how one can apply their creative potential to the greatest extent possible.

What is Creative Intelligence?

Creative Intelligence can be as grand as producing a world-renowned masterpiece, or as mundane as knowing how to solve a routine problem. **Creative Intelligence reflects how we perceive the world around us. It is concerned both with the way we do things and the outcome or result achieved.** An activity can be considered creative if it involves a new or unique approach, and if the results are considered useful and accepted.

Today, Creative Intelligence is determined after the fact. The object here is to determine creative potential without this prior evidence. A test instrument that has been developed can be used to determine a person's "Creative Intelligence." It does this by first exploring their Creative Potential. The test instrument, that will be described in Chapter 2, was based on how people respond to 25 specific questions. The value of the test instrument is that helps us to identify our Creative Intelligence. Too often, this goes unrecognized. The Creative Potential test is similar in design to the Decision Style Inventory that was developed by the author in 1981. That earlier test instrument focused on which occupations correlated with out personality. In that sense, Creative Intelligence also relates to which occupations match our creative ability. A question often raised is whether Mozart and Beethoven would have been great musicians if they did not have pianos readily available to them as children. They obviously had the "potential," but they needed a way to support their talent.

There are many ways that people use their creativity. however, we often make assumptions about how people respond to various opportunities when, in fact, each individual acts and perceives the world from a unique perspective. **Knowing a person's Creative Intelligence helps to predict how they most likely would behave in differing situations**. The test instrument also has the potential of predicting who could be the an inventor, writer or musician.

Why is Creative Intelligence Important?

In an increasingly complex and chaotic world, it is important to expand our focus on creativity. New approaches are needed to cope with the many seemingly unsolvable problems that confront us. We need to be able to deal with issues of global warming, terrorism, violence, homelessness, education and an aging population, to name just a few of the challenges.

With the uncertainty inherent in the world today, there is an opportunity for Creative Intelligence to make an even more significant contribution today than ever before.

Can Creative Intelligence contribute to a quick response to SARS or a cure for cancer? Or how about the ability to save lives with new cardio surgery techniques? All these life-affirming examples also point to the value of Creative Intelligence to society.

A critical problem facing nations today is terrorism. Can creative intelligence help stop another disaster? Like the Space Race of the 1960s, anti-terrorism is our Space Race, for this generation.

Creative solutions often are a direct response to problems that surround us. Creative individuals respond to these problems in different ways. For example, the response to terrorist attacks in recent years has lead to a focus by scientists on various kinds of new safety materials. One innovative result was the development of a material for hardened aircraft containers that can withstand explosions and fires without bursting apart. Called Glare (for glass reinforced), the material absorbs the blast by expanding on impact. At the same time, the fire's heat melts the aluminum core and carbonizes the underlying adhesive bond thus forming a firewall that helps maintain its structural integrity. While Glare's shape will distort under extreme conditions, it will not collapse.

The current challenge is to reduce the weight of the material to be closer to the much lighter weight aluminum. Glare was originally developed by the Delft University of Technology in the Netherlands in response to the Pan Am Flight 103 bombing over Lockerbie, Scotland. Now, however, there is renewed interest in Glare following the terrorist attacks of September 11, 2001 in New York and Washington, D.C., possibly to reinforce cockpit doors on airplanes. This represents the kind of solution that Creative Intelligence can make a reality.

After reading this book, you can expect to have a better understanding of the four areas that will be helpful for your future.

- Learn how to use your Creative Intelligence. This would encourage you to plunge into doing things that utilizes your hidden creative potential.

- Explore the opportunities you could have to apply your creativity. Can you afford to overlook the opportunity of using your creative ability to benefit yourself and others?

- You can help people you know or ones in your organization to utilize their Creative Intelligence.

- Recognize that creativity responds best in an open environment where there is support for creative endeavors.

The future is yours to take or to leave! You can make the choice and exploit your Creative Intelligence or lose the opportunity to contribute to your future and to benefit others.

Acknowledgments

First and foremost, I wish to thank my wife Helen for her patience, support and understanding. The, dedication and understanding of family and colleagues have made this work a meaningful endeavor. Equally vital has been the support of individuals such as Darlene Duran who helped in data gathering for the early version of the Creative Potential Profile and to Robert Tebbe who provided support for data handling in the statistical analysis and Carmen Tebbe for her logistical support.

Thanks to those who generously provided comments, reviews, support and much-needed encouragement, but who are in no way responsible for the material used or errors that have escaped diligent efforts to find them. These include Dr. Jack Alcalay, Dr. Warren Bennis, Stephen Bollenbach, Dr. James Boulgarides, Louis Columbus, Tom Cummings, Dr. Robert Dockson, Walter Gardner, Murdoch Heideman, Mona Kanter, Dr. Kathleen Reardon, Collin Keenan, Dr. Richard Mann, Dr. Gerry Nadler, Dr. Burt Nanus, Jim Paisley, Kimberly Peese, Dr. Ken Robinson, and Gerry Trzanowski.

Special appreciation and thanks goes to Sandy Smith whose intellectual ability and capable support helped make this book a reality. The editors were incredible in pointing out how to make the book more valuable for the reader. Their response was almost instantaneous and invariably on target. Special thanks to Tim Moore who recognized the potential of the subject and encouraged the transformation from the original manuscript to what is now "Creative Intelligence." Russ Hall was especially diligent in reviewing all the revisions of the material. Production supervisor Wil Mara, along with all the reviewers, including Kathy Levinson, Louis Columbus, Gerald Nadler, and Ken Robinson, each added their "Creative Intelligence" that has helped to make this book more readable and useful.

1 ———————————————————

FINDING OUR CREATIVE INTELLIGENCE

"A mind that is stretched to a new idea never returns to its original dimensions."

—*Oliver Wendell Holmes*

Why Is the Study of Creativity Critical?

The survival of planet Earth may well depend on our ability to be more creative. But, how do we gain acceptance of creative ideas, and how do we encourage those who are creative to exercise their ability? To move ahead in our chaotic world, we need to encourage and support this valuable talent. Creativity is basic to making our society viable. Without it, we could easily revert to the way in which our ancestors lived or regress to the way in which many of the underdeveloped parts of the world exist.

Without creativity and innovation in business, we would lose our competitive edge. Every facet of our existence depends to an increasing extent on our utilizing people's creative ability. We need to recognize that most people have creative potential and encourage its use.

In looking at the major innovations and changes in the 20th Century, H. Zuckerman found that they have accelerated what is happening in our world. The airplane, telephone, electricity, automobile, and the move from rural to urban locations are some of the new realities. Who could have predicted the impact that these changes would have in our society? Considering that it took two to three weeks to cross the Atlantic, we now wince at a six- or eight-hour flight across the ocean. There are more cell phones today than people communicating by writing, and this is indicative of what we might anticipate in the future. We now talk about bionic chip implants that can monitor our medical condition, and in the case of diabetes or Parkinson's disease, such an implant may dispense the medication that keeps people alive.

From another perspective, Arthur Schlesinger Jr. talks of moving from exclusion to inclusion, as our experience is no longer dependent on what we witness with our own eyes. We are connected all over the globe by a worldwide information-based economy, and the future is difficult to predict because scientific information is doubling every 2.5 years. Imagine what life will be like just two years from now. Some say it will be based on nanotechnology, with our communication changing so radically that it will challenge the Internet.

What, Then, Is Creativity?

Over the years, many descriptions of creativity have been based on observing individuals and their behavior. However, there is no simple, all-inclusive definition. The perspective here is that creativity is a reflection of our *Creative Intelligence*. In turn, our Creative Intelligence describes how we see and understand the world, our basic beliefs, and our personality. *Creative Intelligence* **differs from what is normally considered General Intelligence. Creativity focuses on how we think and our strong desire to achieve something new or different.**

The Creativity Potential Profile test instrument is used to identify the following four basic styles of Creative Intelligence:

The Four Styles of Creative Intelligence

1. **Intuitive**—Focuses on results and relies on past experience to guide actions.

2. **Innovative**—Concentrates on problem-solving, is systematic, and relies on data.

3. **Imaginative**—Is able to visualize opportunities, is artistic, enjoys writing, and thinks "out of the box."

4. **Inspirational**—Focuses on social change and the giving of self toward that end.

The following describes these four styles of Creative Intelligence in more depth and gives some examples of typical people who exhibit each style:

Intuitive

This style focuses on results and relies on past experience to guide decisions. *Jack Welch*, past Chief Executive Officer (CEO) of General Electric (GE), is an example of this style. He revitalized a stagnant company and was a tough, but charismatic leader. He was hard-working and competitive. Unlike many CEOs, he focused on action and results. He has been described as a "take-no-prisoners, tough guy," "Neutron Jack," and the "world's most ruthless manager." On the other hand, there are stories of his generosity toward and personal concern for individuals in his organization. He was always fair, but tough with rivals. He believed that people were the key to running a successful business and acted on that philosophy to turn GE into a highly success-ful and profitable business. Welch didn't like to use the word "effi-ciency." He believed that creativity was crucial, and he believed that every person had potential.

Innovative

This style concentrates on problems and data and is very systematic. Innovative individuals are willing to work hard and insist on precise and careful experiments. This style is typical of a scientist, engineer, or an inventor such as *Thomas Edison*. *Marie Curie*, another example of an innovator, was a scientist who was working with her husband when she discovered radium and polonium. She was awarded two Nobel Prizes. She persevered in the face of many difficulties, had an excellent mem-ory, and was totally immersed in her work. Although the working envi-ronment often affects how people perform, truly creative people like Marie Curie transcend physical discomfort and inconvenience to pursue their goals and visions. For years she endured a freezing and dilapidated lab in Paris to pursue the work she felt was so important. She believed that perseverance and self-confidence were needed to attain goals. Above all, she was a person who fame did not corrupt.

Imaginative

This style describes people who are artistic, enjoy writing, are good leaders, and can readily visualize opportunities. *Winston Churchill* is an example of a strong, imaginative leader who inspired others. He was the prime minister of Great Britain during World War II and wrote many books about history. He had a unique intellect, a remarkable vitality, and was a prolific writer and artist. He demonstrated great courage in times of crisis and possessed the ability to transmit confi-dence and resolve to others while maintaining his sense of humor.

Although Churchill was one of the world's greatest leaders, he didn't do well in school because he wouldn't study anything he didn't consider relevant. He dropped out of Harrow, but later graduated from the Royal Military College at Sandhurst. It was as a young officer in India that he pursued a course of self-study by reading crates of books shipped to him by his mother. Always mindful of history, he devoured the literature of history and science. His powerful, original intellect was fueled by remarkable vitality. He had great courage and was at his best in times of crisis. Churchill believed, as did *Charles Darwin*, that all life is a struggle, and that chance of survival favors the fittest. Churchill claimed that there were no limits to the ingenuity of man if properly applied under appropriate conditions.

Inspirational

This style focuses on introducing social change and willingly gives of one's self toward that end. *Martin Luther King, Jr.*, who believed in nonviolent protest, was a charismatic leader of the 1960s Civil Rights Movement. He had a stirring oratorical ability and skillfully used nonviolent protest to bring about social change. He was considered a visionary leader. He stressed education as a necessity for intensive and critical thought. King was a master of the language and had a wisdom that characterizes truly visionary leaders. He was awarded the Nobel Peace Prize in 1964; he was the youngest recipient in the history of that prize. He was *Time* Magazine's Man of the Year. King worked tirelessly to bring about the passage of the Voting Rights Act in 1965. Although he was frequently jailed, he considered incarceration a way to show his suffering and willingness to sacrifice himself. Not long before he was assassinated, he said that you have to be willing to die for a cause or else you aren't fit to live it.

Although each of these people were described as being strong in a specific Creative Intelligence style, **most of us have more than one creative style.** For example, Michelangelo was innovative (an engineer and scientist), imaginative (an artist), and intuitive (a sculptor who produced great statues). In addition to the four basic styles that constitute our profile, we can have different levels of intensity for each individual style. Thus, Michelangelo was "strongest" in the innovative category and "strong" in both the imaginative and the intuitive categories. As seen in the example of Michelangelo, the level of intensity for each style results in a pattern for each individual. This approach to creativity expands the possible number of Creative Intelligence styles. The importance of having many styles of creativity is that one is able to more fully and accurately describe an individual's Creative Intelligence.

How Do We Identify a Person's Creative Intelligence?

To understand Creative Intelligence, we need to start with the Creative Potential Profile. It is a test that identifies the styles of Creative Intelligence that best describe an individual. This test instrument is described in detail in Chapter 2.

Creative Intelligence refers to the way individuals use their creative potential. More specifically, **Creative Intelligence describes the aspects of personality that drive us to achieve outstanding results. It also covers how we see and understand the world around us. It deals with our basic values in terms of what we consider right and wrong, or good and bad. And finally, it covers our willingness to take risks.** Edison had the drive to spend endless hours trying to find a filament for light bulbs. He had a basic understanding of the problems with which he was working and was willing to hire top engineers to help carry out his projects. He was so obsessed with the use of electricity that he built a power plant to generate direct current (DC) electricity. Unfortunately, shortly after it was completed, alternating current (AC) electricity was introduced, which made DC electricity obsolete and Edison died broke.

An important consideration in defining Creative Intelligence is that creative results can be as mundane as fixing something to work better or as exotic as painting the *Mona Lisa*. Creative Intelligence, then, covers the way we do things and the outcome or result achieved. We also need to recognize that creative people have a driving passion for their work. Einstein observed that the daily struggle for finding answers arises from an inner need, not from a program or purpose. In a letter to Max Planck, he likened the emotional state of a great achievement to that experienced by a worshipper or lover.

When we consider who is creative, too often we ignore people such as the general who encourages courageous action from his soldiers, the surgeon who develops a new life-saving technique, or the manager who guides his or her organization in the generation of economic wealth. All occupations and all individuals can perform creative acts. By not recognizing that all individuals can be creative, we wind up losing valuable, and in some cases critical, talent.

In the past, people were classified as being creative or not being creative. What a tragic approach to understanding people and their potential contributions! Most people exhibit creative potential, especially when we consider the many ways in which creativity can be expressed.

General Intelligence vs. Creative Intelligence

The relationship between General Intelligence and creativity remains controversial. Creativity depends on how we see the world, our background knowledge in a field, and our curiosity. Current thinking suggests that General Intelligence enables some types of creativity, but it does not necessarily promote or ensure all types of creativity. Creative Intelligence, on the other hand, is expansive, innovative, inventive, unconstrained, daring, uninhibited, fanciful, imaginative, unpredictable, revolutionary, and free-spirited. General Intelligence, which is normally referred to as the Intelligence Quotient, or IQ, is characterized as being focused, disciplined, logical, constrained, down-to-earth, realistic, practical, staid, dependable, and conservative. Both approaches rely on how people view the world, how they respond to various needs or challenges, and their willingness to take risks.

Recent studies in genetics and intelligence have shown that heredity plays a significant role in determining levels of General Intelligence. The influence of genetics on specific cognitive abilities (the way we perceive and understand information) increases with age. Scientists who were looking for the genes that determine our various abilities announced in 1998 the discovery of the first gene to be directly linked with general cognitive ability. In addition to genetic factors, they also looked at biological factors such as micro-neurons in the brain and the effects of hormones. Their conclusion was that most people are capable of creativity in some form, and that creativity is not limited to an elite few. Other scientists studying the brain and its inner workings hope to find the physiological roots of imagination and insight based on examining patients who had brain surgery.

Finding meaning and interpreting experience within a framework of ideas and beliefs are difficult tasks. We tend to create the world in which we live through symbolic thought, like when we say, "What a beautiful painting," or "What a wonderful friend." Our interaction with others and the environment involves the use of words, images, sounds, movements, and gestures. Furthermore, our ability to interpret information, store it mentally, retrieve it, and, under new conditions, apply it, often depends on our Creative Intelligence.

Howard Gardner, who spent two decades studying gifted children and victims of brain damage, concluded that people have multiple kinds of intelligence that they use to varying degrees. He identified eight different kinds of intelligence that relate to people's abilities: linguistic, musical, spatial, bodily, interpersonal, intrapersonal, logical-mathematical, and natural. He viewed the brain as a major determinant of intelligence and correlated different areas of the brain to his eight kinds of intelligence.

In a study done at the Institute of Personality Assessment, it was found that in individuals with an IQ of 120 or higher that General Intelligence was not a significant factor contributing to creativity. The study found that motivation was a key element needed to be creative. This is consistent with the definition of Creative Intelligence, in which personality determines the drive needed to accomplish great things.

Jacob Getzels' research on creativity helped to redefine General Intelligence. He challenged the notion that General Intelligence was all-inclusive. In one of his experiments with high-IQ children, tests were administered for associating words, solving problems of how things are used, finding hidden shapes, and making up stories. He concluded that IQ tests alone did not accurately predict who was creative. What he found was that creative students focused on finding the right problems, not just the right answers. Yale University's Robert Sternberg, well known in the field of creativity, maintains that IQ in general plays less of a role in life than do personality, motivation, experience, social, and economic factors.

What About Our Ancestors?

In their ongoing search for the first creative humans, archeologists discovered the Chauvet Cave in France, which contains paintings that are 35,000 years old. The paintings of animals in the cave employ subtle shading and the use of perspective. This discovery contradicts the theory that artistic technique had a slow progression from primitive to sophisticated art over many thousands of years. Considering that their main concern was survival, our ancestor's digression into art demonstrates that the need to be creative is a natural instinct.

There are many examples of the early inventiveness of humans. Considering the limited exposure to all the tools we have today, our

ancestors were brilliant problem-solvers who discovered and implemented a wide variety of applications. A brief sample of what they
were able to accomplish includes:

- Rudimentary calendars were used in France, 1300 B.C.

- Plastic surgery was performed in India in the 1st Century B.C.

- China used flame-throwers in the 10th Century.

- Baghdad had an efficient postal service, banks, and a paper mill
  in medieval times.

No one knows who was first to recognize that the flowing water of
rivers could be used as a means of transport, or that a log rolling down
an incline would be the precursor to the wheel. Domesticated animals
replaced some of the need for brute force, along with knives and plows
and other tools that progressively relieved the burden on humans. These
innovations allowed humans to turn from a focus on work to a greater
use of their intellect to solve problems. For example, the laws of physics
and contributions of mathematicians, such as those from Sir Isaac Newton, provided the foundation of what we use today in those fields.

The progress of humanity over the centuries has led to a greater
use of our Creative Intelligence. It is an extraordinarily powerful
attribute of humans. When encouraged, it can literally change the
growth of civilizations.

There are many examples throughout world history where Creative
Intelligence contributed to change. The printing press completely
changed the political structure of nations and provided the ability to
transmit knowledge more easily. Today, the Internet, air travel, and
ease of obtaining material via electronic means continue to bring about
significant change in our society.

Can We Measure Creative Intelligence?

We cannot see, hear, or observe creative potential. Only after the fact can we judge whether a person has been creative. However, a way to determine creative potential without any prior evidence, as mentioned earlier, is by the use of a test instrument called the Creative Potential Profile. It is able to reveal an individual's Creative Intelligence. The value of a test instrument is that it helps us to easily identify each person's Creative Intelligence. However, simply knowing our potential is not enough. Circumstances or the environment often prevent the exercise of our potential. For example, not too long ago, a dress code was demanded by organizations; the gray-flannel suit was considered de rigueur in business. Other organizations would not allow employees to mix socially unless they were similar in rank.

An important focus of this book is to show how we can find our Creative Intelligence and thereby use our latent talents. Most people go through life without ever knowing their creative potential. Too often, people take jobs out of economic necessity rather than matching their occupation to their true creative potential. **The Creative Potential Profile test instrument can help you find your "hidden potential." With this knowledge, you will be in a better position to determine how to spend your life. Many gifted people miss this opportunity because they lack that knowledge.**

A question often raised is: Can I change my creative profile? In general, the answer is that, genetically, we are who we are. We can improve or enhance our ability, but that does not change our personality or our underlying need or drive to perform creative activities. Another issue is one described by *The Economist*, which mentions how poorly students are doing in math and science. Perhaps, instead of being critical of the students, we should try to find out the root cause. Is it lack of interest or is it lack of understanding? Educators rarely consider that each of us has a different Creative Intelligence that affects how we view various subjects in school. A review of Winston

Churchill's life shows that he was largely self-taught because he had no interest in certain subjects. Or, it may be that teachers focus on the students' ability to do well in class rather than on other abilities. We can improve education, but, as will be shown later in the book, we need new ways of "explaining" subject matter so that it is understandable by all.

When possible, we tend to pursue endeavors that match our Creative Intelligence. If we are in an appropriate environment, it tends to stimulate otherwise nascent talent. George Gershwin played an old piano that was in his home and became a virtuoso. He had the talent, but he needed a means to develop his potential. So, can people change who they are? To some extent they can. Through education, encouragement, and support, we can provide an environment that allows people to experiment and "find" themselves. We can also utilize professional psychological support to assist in overcoming personality problems. But, we all have innate abilities, personalities, values, and so on, and we need to learn to live with who we are.

What are the underlying factors that shape our creative potential? There are several ways of answering this question. One approach is to review how famous people behaved. What were they like and what did they have in common? These and similar questions will be examined by studying a number of well-known individuals to determine which underlying factors or conditions helped them succeed.

What Is the Creative Potential Profile?

The Creative Potential Profile is a test instrument that measures an individual's preference for each of four basic Creative Intelligence styles. The instrument has undergone a careful statistical analysis to assure that what it predicts is accurate and reliable. The results have been very positive. For example, approximately 80% of people who were asked, "Do you agree with your profile?" answered yes. Individuals who retook the test were surprised to find that their preferences for creative activity remained the same. This kind of analysis provides us with the confidence that the Creative Potential Profile is a reliable test instrument. **The real value of a test instrument, however, is its ability to "predict" whether a person really has the Creative Intelligence style that was identified by the test.** To date, the results for the Creativity Potential Profile have been well above accepted psychological standards.

To assure that the Creative Potential Profile would be accurate, the design was based on the same approach as a prior test instrument developed by the author. That test instrument, the Decision Style Inventory, was used to measure an individual's personality and to predict which occupations the person would find most satisfying. That test has a 95% predictive validity. In critical decisions, such as the selection of a president for a major corporation, it has proven to be invaluable. The choice of a director for a major port was based on the test results along with other information. There are numerous examples showing its high level of predictability.

The Creative Potential Profile described here is the test instrument that is used to identify the four basic styles of Creative Intelligence. This approach to dealing with creativity is more realistic than simply considering people as being creative or not creative.

Other Views of Creativity

An important consideration in understanding creativity is that it can be positive or negative. Unfortunately, creativity is not always applied in a positive way. Look at the approach to creative accounting used at Enron and other major corporations to give a false picture of earnings. Terrorists also applied their creative ability in using fully loaded airplanes as bombs in the attacks on the World Trade Center. Can we prevent these occurrences? Perhaps if we apply our creative abilities, we can find the root cause for their discontent and help to alleviate the underlying reasons that lead to their actions, such as the poverty in many parts of the world.

Creative Intelligence incorporates creative mobility and insight when understanding problems. For instance, the chemical structure of benzene came from an insightful dream about coiled snakes. Creative insights, generally, are the result of relaxing the mind so that new possibilities can be considered. There literally is no limit to new ideas or answers to difficult problems if we are sufficiently motivated to find them. Creative individuals must be willing to confront adversity, question authority, and boldly go beyond what is expected of them. Creative minds have the imagination that allows them to see, with their "mind's eye," images, people, and other thoughts that are not actually present, not happening at the moment, or not even real. Imagination goes beyond the simple recall of images from reality and can involve hypothetical, fanciful, or unusual possibilities invented by the mind. These, in turn, have led to many of the inventions we now enjoy.

Who, Then, Is Creative?

By examining what creative people have been able to accomplish, we have another basis for identifying Creative Intelligence. Creative people are dedicated to what they do and have the drive and passion to bring their endeavors to fruition. Society, unfortunately, very often considers creative people dreamers or visionaries. Socrates suffered because of his use of critical thinking and unwavering commitment to the truth. When sentenced to death, he chose to drink hemlock and died with his friends and students around him.

There is little question that the future depends on those who dare to dream and who believe strongly enough to make those dreams a reality, such as Thomas Edison, who would not give up until he found the answer for the light bulb. **Who will next create some new device**

or approach that will radically change how we live? Will it be someone like Thomas Edison with his practical system to harness electricity, and his inventions such as the phonograph and motion-picture camera? Or will it be someone like Bob Dutcher, who had what seemed like a "harebrained" idea to use a water jet to "blast" blood clots out of clogged arteries in the heart? His invention, the Angiojet, removes blood clots in the critical seconds that often mean the difference between life and death.

Examples of creative individuals illustrate the complexity of determining how people use their Creative Intelligence. Stephen Wolfram, thought by some to have the greatest scientific mind of our age, has developed a theory of how the universe works. The book in which he presents his theory to the world is titled *A New Kind of Science*. He sees it as a world-changing book, in league with Newton's *Principia* and Darwin's *Origin of the Species*.

Stephen Wolfram's genius was recognized very early. Born in London in 1959, he entered Eton College at age 13, wrote a book on particle physics at 14, and published a paper in the field of nuclear physics at 17. After a year at Oxford University, he went to work at Argonne National Laboratory in the Theoretical High-Energy Physics Group. The summer he turned 18, he published a paper on heavy quark production that became a classic in the field. The next year, Nobel Prize winner Murray Gell-Mann invited Wolfram to the California Institute of Technology (Cal Tech). At Cal Tech, he continued to produce remarkable work and was awarded the MacArthur "Genius" Fellowship at 21 for the "breadth of his thinking." In the late 1980s, Wolfram developed a groundbreaking mathematical software program called *Mathematica*.

Another example of an extraordinary individual is classical composer Ludwig von Beethoven. He developed his musical talent by study and often duplication of others' works. His first works came from practice, imitation, and learning from what had been done before. Beethoven kept his thoughts with him for long periods of time. He claimed that he never forgot a theme and described his work ethic as continuously changing what he was doing until he was satisfied. At that point, he would elaborate on what he had been working. He claimed that the underlying idea of a theme never left him. Rather, it would grow as he envisioned what he would do with it. Beethoven was described as being reclusive and cranky, which adds to the picture of a sometimes-difficult genius. Yet he would respond to criticism by changing his music to a simpler form. For example, he replaced one musically challenging piece with a short allegro. Today, Beethoven's *Ninth Symphony* has brought tears to people's eyes and has become a symbol of classical music.

In the business world, Bill Gates started with a small software contract and a dream that computers would be on every desk in offices and homes. He pursued this line of thinking, and it eventually led to the formation of the Microsoft Corporation. His ideas helped fuel the information technology revolution, and along the way, he became one of the richest men in the world. Thomas Edison had a dream about using electricity, and he became one of the world's most prolific inventors, leaving a legacy of hundreds of useful products.

Environmental Influences on Creativity

The social or organizational context in which one works can directly affect creativity. Fredrick Chopin, at the age of seven, had already authored two polonaises. As a child prodigy, he was featured in the Warsaw newspapers and performed at receptions for visiting dignitaries. He extended his interests when he first heard folk music at peasant weddings. He was struck with their distinct tonality and richness of rhythms. In part, his fame was a result of melodic invention and brilliant effects along with perfect harmony.

In 1837, Chopin met and entered into a close relationship with French writer George Sand. She provided Chopin with great tenderness and warmth. They soon became lovers, and spent much time together. The period he spent with Sand was considered the happiest and most productive of his outstanding career. The relationship lasted for almost 11 years. His separation from Sand in 1848 led to a breakdown in his health and he died soon thereafter. Chopin would probably have been known as a marvelous composer without Sand, but the supportive environment she provided added another dimension to his music that might easily have been lost.

Theresa Amabile was one of the early researchers who recognized the importance of the environment and how personality, drive, and motivation affect the creative process. She found that improvement in performance usually resulted when creativity was encouraged. She also found that creativity depended on using skills relevant to a problem at hand, building on one's expertise and talent in a specific field. Creative Intelligence is consistent with her description of creativity. She claimed that creative individuals were not judgmental, were willing to take risks, and would pursue their ideas for long periods of time because they were strongly motivated to complete what they had started.

In her studies of children, she found that they exhibited creative behavior when they were significantly different from others and achieved meaningful goals. A three-year-old teaching herself how to tie her shoes by experimenting, without help or training, was considered innovative. Imaginative behavior included drawings that contained a play on words, such as a rainbow raining bowties. Gifted children were generally considered creative. On the other hand, children with high IQs were not always creative. Children who learned by watching and copying demonstrated General Intelligence, but not necessarily creativity.

Kinds of Creativity

Creativity is not limited to any one field. People with high Creative Intelligence have the potential to produce significant results in a

number of fields. The people below cover the many fields in which one can be creative:

- A scientist who found unexpected results—*Marie Curie*

- An inventor who persisted against the odds—*Thomas Edison*

- A great artist who was not appreciated during his lifetime—*Vincent Van Gogh*

- A child prodigy whose music has enchanted us for over 200 years—*Wolfgang Mozart*

- A leader whose self-sacrifice changed a nation—*Mohandas Gandhi*

- A mathematician who changed the world of science—*Albert Einstein*

- A sculptor/artist who inspired untold numbers of people—*Michelangelo*

- A blind person who could "read" others—*Helen Keller*

- An artisan who has not been surpassed to this day—*Antonio Stradivarius*

- A dancer who epitomized elegance—*Fred Astaire*

- An educator who achieved the impossible with students in math—*Jaime Escalante*

What did each of these individuals have in common?

- Each had extraordinary accomplishments.

- Each demonstrated unusual talent or ability.

- Each persisted in his/her endeavors.

- Each found unique approaches to his/her effort.

- Each had knowledge or understanding that others lacked.

- Each was willing to take risks and introduce change.

- Each had the drive to go beyond what was expected.

- Each had the courage to question the status quo.

- Each was able to visualize new possibilities.

What an exciting world we would have if our Creative Intelligence could be unlocked, especially when we consider that creative ability is not dependent on high IQ, nor is it limited to any specific field.

The Many Faces of Creativity

A number of researchers have suggested that there are multiple kinds of creativity. For example, Howard Gardner has identified five types of individuals who exhibit creativity: problem-solvers, theory-builders, artists and inventors, ritualized workers, and social activists. As can be seen, research by Gardner and others supports the case for multiple categories of creativity. Interestingly, Gardner's categories are comparable to the styles used to describe Creative Intelligence.

It is obvious from the many views of creativity that it is a broad subject and should not be confined to a limited set of behaviors or activities. In many instances, creativity has initially been rejected, ignored, or even belittled. Vincent Van Gogh only sold one painting in his lifetime to his brother Theo, and Alexander Graham Bell was laughed at during his first public demonstration of the telephone. Unfortunately, the world frequently fails to embrace creativity because it is different or new. Although creativity does not depend on recognition by others, ultimately, to be of value, it needs to be accepted.

There are many reasons why change is difficult and creativity is impeded. Foremost is a non-receptive environment—"If it ain't broke, don't fix it!" Or managers who fear or resent change and will not tolerate any new approach that might challenge their authority. For example, at Easy Washing Machine, a new approach was suggested by one of the engineers that could save the company 10% in shipping costs. It required using a new part to hold the machine in place during assembly. The foreman tried the new part and found it difficult to use. He rejected the new idea by saying, "We've been doing shipping this way for 20 years and I'm not changing now." Not too long after this incident, a new type of washing machine was introduced in the industry that made the Easy machine obsolete, perhaps a victim of its unwillingness to change.

Factors that stifle creativity and innovation include tradition. At Easy Washing Machine, it could have been an unwillingness to try the unknown, fear of the loss of power, or an environment that prevented change. It is sad that people in power often control the future without regard for the consequences.

The Role of Personality in Creativity

Many factors influence or motivate people to do things. Personality appears to be a major driving force that strongly influences people's behavior. Personality affects how we view the world and what is important to us. Sir Isaac Newton had the ability to concentrate on the same problem for long stretches of time—from hours to weeks, or longer—until he had a solution. He wrote that it was during his most productive periods that he thought constantly about the problems on which he was working. Certain personality types seem to require that kind of passionate immersion in creative activity, to the exclusion of other concerns.

In her study of creativity, Jane Piirto considers personality a major factor contributing to the success of productive, creative people. She identifies the following key personality attributes that contribute to creativity: being imaginative, having insight or intuition, being open and perceptive, being willing to take risks, and having a high tolerance for ambiguity. These attributes help creative people deal with the many unknowns they face. Although these personality characteristics may be innate in highly creative people, Piirto feels that some of the behaviors can be taught to individuals who have creative potential.

In his studies of the creative process, David Perkins claims that it is not mysterious. Mental leaps that solve problems in a flash are actually part of a process that has many logical steps. The thought process does not follow a simple path. Rather, a mental leap generally is the result of a great deal of thinking that finds a solution in a very short period of time. Creative individuals often notice opportunities and search their memories for relevant information. They then form judgments based on close observation as work progresses. Another consideration is that taking a break from a problem can provide valuable creative insight. Afterward, creative individuals return to the problem renewed and refreshed.

An intriguing aspect of creativity is that it is everywhere, and creative individuals rarely know the exact source of their ideas. Creativity arises from being open, and from noticing and remembering. A critical question concerns how to recognize the value of new ideas. Most individuals generate many new or novel ideas, but acceptance of those ideas is what determines their real worth. Consider how many scientists, artists, and writers were ridiculed or ignored, only to be rediscovered years later and then recognized as having made significant contributions. Vincent Van Gogh and Emily Dickinson are classic examples.

Careful observation and research are just as important to artists as to scientists, although they take a different form. Artists study the mechanics of their craft and pay close attention to the way they can best describe what they have seen. Inspiration often arises from unlikely sources, from seemingly unrelated happenings or observations. A lifetime of immersion in museums, theaters, music, literature, and enjoying the beauty of nature provides both a framework and perspective for the aspiring artist.

Einstein often played with what he called "thought experiments" as he went about his daily life. When he was 16, he looked at a sunbeam that he imagined was moving at the speed of light and wondered about the effect such speed would have on his perceptions of the world around him. The solution did not come to him for nearly a decade, when the pieces fell into place in his mind when waking one morning. He sent his theory off to *The Annals of Physics* after working on it for only a few weeks. His basic hypothesis was that the speed of light was absolute, and space and time were relative. The theory that seemed so intuitive to him stirred great controversy among physicists. Interestingly, recent studies have shown that there actually can be small variations in the absolute speed of light.

Einstein's breakthrough required a high level of Creative Intelligence that utilized his mathematical ability. It involved a combination of intuition, rationality, and innovation that transformed the understanding of physics and led to the atomic age.

Such breakthroughs have moved knowledge forward at many points in human history. Where do these creative moments come from? Thinkers and scientists have pondered that question over the centuries. Such moments are generally independent of conscious control, but are most likely to come when the mind is receptive. Mozart said that his best ideas came when he was completely alone and in a good mood. He went on to say that it was on those occasions that his ideas flowed best. Interestingly, he did not know where he found his ideas, but he recognized that they could not be forced.

An anecdote about Thomas Edison supplies yet another example of how creative individuals behave. Edison, along with his friend, Cyrus Eaton, suffered from significant hearing loss. Eaton asked him why he didn't perfect a hearing aid. Edison responded by saying he wasn't interested in hearing that much.

Can We Really Understand Creativity?

Harvard University's David Perkins disagrees with the myth that creativity magically pops up out of nowhere. Perkins, a co-director of Project Zero, has studied the cognitive skills of artists and scientists. He believes that personality and personal values have a significant role in determining an individual's creative potential. Based on over 40 years of studying scientists and artists, Perkins has identified six characteristics of the creative mind in his Snowflake Model of Creativity: Some scientists believe we may never fully understand the creative process. On the other hand, a number of creativity researchers have made progress toward a comprehensive psychology of creativity. Many hope that learning more about creativity will give us a way to find solutions to important problems and questions that confront us.

1. Creative people have a strong commitment based on a strong belief in what they do.

2. They have a need to create order and meaning in what appears chaotic.

3. Artists spend enormous amounts of time and energy to express their vision of the world.

4. Scientists look through masses of data to find information relevant to their theory.

This kind of behavior was typical of Einstein, who even went so far as to use one type of soap for everything so that he could focus his energies on more important matters. Creative individuals also have the ability to identify problems by asking the right questions and are willing to go beyond the boundaries of a given field of knowledge. Linus Pauling suggested that using critical judgment can help one to know when to toss out bad ideas. **Creative individuals have mental mobility, which allows them to find new or innovative approaches to problems and to evaluate opposing positions, plus they are willing to risk failure.** Interestingly, geniuses can produce mediocre work along with their breakthrough discoveries and successes. Creative individuals constantly seek stimulation and excitement.

Creative people are not always objective. However, to test their ideas, they do not restrict their view of the world. As an example, poets who have accepted critical reviews have often produced better work than those who didn't. Creative people often need to set their ego aside and consult with colleagues to test their ideas. Additionally, creative individuals have a strong inner motivation, drive, or spiritual need. One key to understanding creativity is to recognize that the inner drive and passion to create for its own sake are what matter, not external rewards. Those who focus on external rewards generally are less successful than those who are driven to create regardless of what the world thinks. Creative endeavors provide the inner motivations of enjoyment, satisfaction, and challenge.

The creative process builds on preparation, incubation, illumination, and verification to achieve meaningful results. Preparation requires learning and memory, while incubation and illumination require intellectual freedom, risk-taking, and a tolerance for ambiguity. Intuition has been described as a "mental leap of faith" made by creative individuals that allows them to make choices even when there is incomplete information. Often, creative individuals are willing to pursue a course of action that contradicts conventional wisdom and accepted theories. Overall, **creative people know *"how"* to think—using their Creative Intelligence—instead of *"what"* to think about.**

A mind not utilized to its full capacity is a cruel injustice for both the individual and for society. **If we are able to determine an individual's creative potential and are willing to support the individual, we can expect that he/she will achieve the extraordinary. In too many cases, organizations impose constraints that limit an individual's ability to find answers to complex problems, to invent new products, to conduct research, or to create works of art or music. Constraints are also built into educational systems that maintain traditional approaches to teaching and fail to take into account our**

Creative Intelligence. Fortunately, creative individuals are able to draw inferences from data they have studied. This helps them to understand complex processes and to make accurate judgments regarding how to proceed with their research.

A key objective of this book is to assist you in identifying your Creative Intelligence potential. There may be areas of endeavor that you might consider if you knew your Creative Intelligence style. **Too often, we overlook our creative potential because we do not know our Creative Intelligence style.** With this knowledge, you could find new areas of endeavor that you would find rewarding. For example, a young woman who did not enjoy secretarial work found that she had artistic talent. This knowledge changed her life. She worked with an author of children's books who included her sketches. It was not a financial reward that she attained, but a sense of satisfaction and completeness in her life. She now has a way of looking at herself that can guide her in understanding what would be most satisfying for the rest of her life.

Some people think that they know what they want to be. The Creative Potential Profile provides reinforcement for their thinking. Obviously, the test alone is not the answer to questions this complex. However, the knowledge provides a way of looking at some of the difficult questions we all face.

2

FINDING YOUR CREATIVE POTENTIAL

Somebody said it couldn't be done,
But he with a chuckle replied
That "maybe it couldn't" but he would be one
Who wouldn't say no, till he'd tried.
So he buckled right in, with the trace of a grin
On his face. If he worried he hid it.
He started to sing as he tackled the thing
That couldn't be done, and he did it.

—Edgar Guest

Why Is Creativity Important?

Throughout human history, creativity has been the subject of interpretation and speculation. The scientific study of creativity is a fairly recent phenomenon. J. Paul Guilford, at the University of Southern California, produced a testing program for the military in World War II that was widely used for measuring creativity. With such a tool, it seemed that it would be only a matter of time before creativity could be measured as accurately as intellectual ability.

In the past, people believed that creativity was a mysterious concept and impossible to define in specific terms. While that may have

27

been true, the behavior of creative individuals is indeed observable and has been the subject of meaningful study. Jane Piirto's research studies on creativity and found that it is a natural activity. She also found that it is based on an individual's personality as well as described in Chapter 1. Genetic and environmental factors, the home environment, school and community, and chance events all affect our creative behavior.

The value of knowing our Creative Intelligence is that it can help us deal with the changing world in which we live. Ambiguity rules in today's world. What we have taken for granted over the years no longer seems to apply. From a chaotic economy, to travel problems, to personal freedom, and many others, everything is more uncertain than ever before. Where will the next terrorist attacks occur, when, and with what type of weapon? How do we deal with an accelerating rate of change in the economy or available resources such as oil? There are no simple answers to these questions because rules are no longer the rule. **To cope with our new environment, we need to be more flexible and adaptive.** If we are more creative, we are in a better position to cope with the problems with which we are confronted.

How Do We Use Creative Intelligence?

Creative Intelligence reflects an inner drive that affects our ability to achieve desired goals. Humans are inherently curious and are constantly looking for answers. It is normal to want to know how things work and how new and better things are created. Inquisitiveness is largely dependent on one's Creative Intelligence. It also reflects how we differ from one another and how we respond to various situations. We judge an individual as being friendly if we observe that kind of behavior in a variety of situations, especially difficult ones. Creative Intelligence likewise helps to explain individual preferences in the way we use and interpret information and how we apply that knowledge to new situations. Individual Creative Intelligence is unique and is based on enduring and stable characteristics over long periods of time.

The discovery of new ideas, theories, or methods provides a high level of satisfaction, but it rarely happens overnight. Michael Michalko looks at creative thinking as comparable to heating solid material until it becomes fluid. In that state, remote ideas are able to combine with other ideas to produce creative interactions. We can facilitate the creative process by allowing greater freedom and interaction in the work environment.

French chemist Louis Pasteur, founder of microbiology and inventor of pasteurization, believed that only a prepared mind led to significant new results. Today, this is called having "domain knowledge," or "knowing the territory." **The creative process depends on knowledge and experience that lead to new knowledge. Knowledge, however, is only a means to an end.** It gives us insight and understanding, which allows our mind to explore extensions to new domains that we might not have considered previously. Delving into new areas can be both exciting and rewarding. Depending on our Creative Intelligence style, for example, the innovative style needs knowledge as a foundation to explore new areas. Without a background in statistics, Florence Nightingale might not have discovered the cause of infections at military hospitals. She found that cleanliness made a significant difference in the survival of wounded soldiers.

Knowledge Can Be Confining

There are times when knowledge becomes a straightjacket and does not allow the freedom to explore beyond what is known. An example is the use of "work sampling" to determine the amount of time a worker is idle. If the worker is idle only a small percentage of the time, the sampling becomes unmanageable. If we violate the correct statistical approach and think out of the box, we would only need a small sample. This approach reduces the time needed to find a reasonable answer. If we insist on statistical accuracy, the cost becomes prohibitive. After all, the information is only needed as a guideline for the work to be done.

B.F. Skinner, an early pioneer in the study of psychological processes, felt that interesting research ideas should be investigated immediately and not set aside for a later time. He felt that a good idea that is put off until later is often lost. The following story presents another perspective on Skinner's premise: A Bell Labs team headed by William Shockley was experimenting with transistors. Along the way, without waiting to finish their other research, as Skinner had suggested, they invented the junction transistor and the integrated circuit along with other breakthroughs that are used today in electronics and computers. Translated, Skinner's idea is "Strike while the iron is hot." Shockley, however, considered that the creative process involved "many failures" along the way to finding new ideas.

Teflon was an accidental discovery made by Roy Plunkett in 1938, when he was working on a new refrigerant. One of his experiments resulted in a white material that conducted heat and failed to stick to other surfaces. He immediately switched gears to study this material and eventually developed it into a highly successful commercial product called Teflon. Similarly, Ray Kroc started the McDonald's franchise system of fast-food restaurants. Based on his business experience, he immediately recognized the potential of the thriving little hamburger stand of the McDonald brothers. They had developed a simple, economical formula for running their business. Kroc became a very wealthy man by adding his own ideas, such as having affordable prices, insisting on extreme cleanliness, and having amusement rides for children.

How We See the World

An important aspect of creativity is our ability to see and understand our environment. **Perception, which is part of Creative Intelligence, is how we see and react to new information**. Human perception actively restructures information that is needed to form a picture of the world. Thus, interpretation is not merely a passive reflection of what is seen. Rather, perception is influenced by memories, which play an important role in the ability to recognize and classify information. Roadblocks to perception can occur when an individual jumps to conclusions rather than questioning a given situation. Information also can be influenced by symptoms rather than the real cause of a problem. This becomes especially important when group values influence what is acceptable.

An individual's past experiences also influence how new information is interpreted. Perception also is affected by our personal needs, values, and emotions. An example of how perception determines what we see is the following description of a visit to a Chinese temple: Entering the temple, one is struck by the fact that the entry hall ends in a blank wall. The steps are off to the left side because "evil spirits cannot turn corners." The guide to the temple shows how scrolls having a person's fortune are selected from a rotating drum. Somewhat sheepishly, the guide says, "I know what you must be thinking." To avoid any embarrassment, one of the tour group members speaks up: "Do you know that music, voices and pictures are floating around in this room?" Surprised and somewhat perplexed, the guide asks, "Where?" The tourists explains, "If you have a portable radio, you can hear voices and music. If you have a portable television, you can see pictures. Just because we can't 'sense' something doesn't mean it is not there." The guide feels more at ease by the explanation that sometimes we need to accept the unknown. In a similar vein, Creative Intelligence in humans is not easily seen or sensed. Rather, we need a definitive means to reveal creative potential such as the Creative Potential Profile test instrument.

Lord Rutherford used the solar system as an analogy to represent the structure of the hydrogen atom. His analogy was not precise, but it provided a useful way to think about atoms. William Gordon developed an approach to finding creative solutions to problems that relied on analogies. He called his process *Synectics*. He started by considering himself as part of a problem to be solved. For instance, he looked at animals to find how they caught prey in order to find ways to build a better mousetrap.

Creative Intelligence describes how our mind uses mental codes, over which we have no control, to determine how information is seen and understood. This helps to explain why each of us comes away with different impressions of what we read, what we see at a play, how we hear music, or how we listen to a poem. Our knowledge and ability to interpret images are what makes memory important. Memory provides us with the capacity to generate new ideas and move beyond personal experiences.

Reasoning describes how our mind deals with new information. Reasoning relates new information to previous ideas. However, reasoning can lead to wrong actions when a problem is not correctly understood. Take, for example, Frank Lorenzo, Chairman of Texas Air, who initiated the buyout of Eastern Airlines. Charles E. Bryan, president of the Eastern Airlines' machinist's union (IAM), was naïve in thinking that he could gain favor with the new owner by sending a warm telegram to Lorenzo. He said that he looked forward to a cooperative relationship. Lorenzo never responded to the telegram. As Chairman of Eastern Airlines, Lorenzo was more interested in making sweeping changes than in a cooperative relationship. His intention was to slash the wages of union members and change existing work rules. Lorenzo believed that work rules inhibited the productivity of union members. He started by attacking Bryan's IAM members. In response, the union refused to reopen its contract. The union's position on part-time mechanics was a thorn in Lorenzo's side, along with his belief that paying baggage handlers and janitors $16 an hour was outlandish considering that it was twice what he paid at Continental Airlines. Lorenzo misjudged the situation, however, and was stunned when the pilots and flight attendants honored the IAM picket line and refused to work.

Cognition and Creativity

Cognition describes our ability to recognize and understand information, ideas, and concepts that are needed to form judgments. **Cognition is important for creativity because it allows us to combine ideas into more complex ones based on past experience.** It also affects our ability to understand new information. **Cognition includes the ability to construct a wide variety of concrete and abstract concepts stemming from seemingly inconsequential information to generate creative ideas.** Writers often produce a complex plot by combining a number of different ideas. Inventors also view different ideas or consider different ways to look at a problem to determine whether a result is really new.

The human mind is indeed a paradox. Perception and cognition are exceedingly complex, but are critical to the creative process. If we fail to respond to stimuli or perceive problems properly, the output can be poor. Furthermore, judgment and personality can prevent or interfere with this process.

Creative Visualization

Our imagination is a critical part of Creative Intelligence because it is a powerful tool that helps us visualize and understand alternatives. Visualization helps us understand unexpected ideas and new possibilities. The creative potential of mental imagery has been demonstrated by many studies. It has been used in laboratory experiments as well as in everyday life, such as for rearranging furniture or designing new products. Creative visualization also helps to overcome mental blocks that interfere with creative thinking. Intuition and insight share some of the same characteristics of visualization by suddenly interrupting our thinking in ways that can contribute to new ideas or understanding.

The Creative Potential Profile

A test instrument called the Creative Potential Profile was developed to determine a person's Creative Intelligence style. The Creative Potential Profile shows an individual's preference for each of the four Creative Intelligence styles. Table 2–1 illustrates how we think and what we

TABLE 2-1   Creative potential diagram.

	INNOVATIVE	**IMAGINATIVE**
Considers Future Opportunities	(Is curious)	(Is insightful)
	Scientist/Engineer/Inventor	*Artist/Musician/ Writer/Leader*
Cognitive	• Uses original approaches • Is willing to experiment • Relies on systematic inquiry	• Willing to take risks • Has leaps of imagination • Is an independent thinker
Complexity	**INTUITIVE**	**INSPIRATIONAL**
	(Is resourceful)	(Is a visionary)
	Manager/Actor/Politician	*Educator/Leader/Writer*
Focuses on Current Needs	• Achieves goals • Uses common sense • Solves problems	• Responds to societal needs • Willingly gives of self • Has courage of convictions
	DIRECT	**BROAD**

VALUES PERSPECTIVE

(What we believe is right or wrong, or good or bad)

value. Thinking can range from simple to complex ideas based on our cognitive complexity. The bottom of the diagram shows an individual's personal values and beliefs. These determine what we consider right and wrong, or desirable and undesirable.

At the top left of Table 2-1, the individual focuses on future opportunities. At the bottom left, the emphasis is on current needs. These categories are broad and intended to describe how our mind responds to creative opportunities.

The lower portion of the diagram shows how we interpret ideas, how we value them or feel about them, and what we feel is important. These are described as direct values in contrast with broad concerns. These descriptions classify creativity into categories that are used as the basis for determining our Creative Intelligence styles.

An overriding consideration beyond cognition and values is the driving force of personality. It is a key factor underlying creativity. Our drive, ability to handle complexity, and basic needs, when combined with what we consider valuable, needed, or desirable, describe the four basic Creative Intelligence styles. Each of these four styles is described below:

Intuitive

This style describes resourceful individuals and is typical of managers, actors, and politicians. The intuitive creative style emphasizes achievement, hard work, and the ability to find good answers quickly; it focuses on results, uses common sense, and relies on past experience.

Innovative

This style describes inquisitive individuals and is typical of scientists, engineers, and inventors. The innovative style emphasizes persistence, experimentation, and careful analysis; it handles complexity with ease.

Imaginative

This style describes insightful individuals and is typical of artists, musicians, writers, and leaders. The imaginative style is able to identify potential opportunities; this style is also willing to take risks by breaking with tradition. In addition, the imaginative style is open-minded and often relies on humor to convey ideas.

Inspirational

This style describes visionary individuals and is typical of educators, leaders, and writers. The inspirational style has a positive, action-oriented outlook on societal needs and is willing to give of self to achieve goals. This style is concerned with introducing change that helps others.

Creative individuals respond to various situations differently based on their Creative Intelligence style. For example, the intuitive style responds quickly to operational problems. On the other hand, innovative individuals rely on a considerable amount of information and take time to study and gain insight into problems. Individuals with the imaginative style use value judgments as the basis for their decisions. They rely on a large volume of data, and take considerable time to think things through because of their need to evaluate options and consequences. They are the people who typically say, "On the one hand, we should do this; but on the other hand, here are the consequences of doing that." This kind of rumination requires time, but generally leads to better and broader solutions than those who jump to conclusions. The last is the inspirational style. These individuals are concerned with the welfare of others and willingly give of themselves. The inspirational style relies on instincts or feelings, and these individuals focus on working with people in correcting organizational or societal problems.

Is any style better than the others? It depends on the situation. In an emergency, the intuitive style makes good, quick decisions, but when it comes to understanding the far-reaching effects of certain problems, the imaginative style will generally be more effective.

Creativity reflects our Creative Intelligence styles. Creativity relies on our cognition (ability to visualize and understand), memory (learned responses), and ability to extend, restate, recombine, or invent new responses to various situations, both internal (drive, risk-taking, etc.) and interacting with the external environment.

The Creative Potential Profile Test Instrument

A test instrument called the Creative Potential Profile was developed as a means to identify a person's creative potential. The Creative Potential Profile in Table 2–2 uses 25 questions for determining the four basic styles of creativity shown in Table 2–1.

The Creative Potential Profile test instrument ranks the relative importance of each of the four responses. Thus, the responses for Question #1 might be: 3,2,1,4. The significance of ranking is to show the preference that an individual has for each of the answers. The scoring of the test starts by adding up the four columns. This provides a "raw score" for the individual taking the test. A computer program has been developed to provide an interpretation of the meaning of the raw scores. Based on the raw scores, the program shows what is important and how the style can be used.

The test is found on the next two pages.
A scoring chart is on the page following.

TABLE 2-2   Creative Potential Profile, Version 5.1.

For each question, place a [1] in the box following the answer that is MOST like you, a [2] for the answer that is MODERATELY like you, a [3] for the answer that is a LITTLE like you, and a [4] for the answer that is LEAST like you.

1. I often wonder how to	introduce change	discover new solutions	make ideas exciting	work best with people
2. My strength is being	decisive	thorough	imaginative	understanding
3. Successful people are	ambitious	disciplined	willing to take risks	self-confident
4. I get my best results by	focusing on current problems	applying careful analysis	trying new approaches	gaining the support of others
5. I see the future as	unknown	a challenge	providing many opportunities	facilitating change
6. I appreciate teachers who	explain ideas clearly	make learning interesting	recognize original ideas	involve others in learning
7. People see me as	energetic	persistent	a perfectionist	committed
8. People who make things happen	are highly motivated	enjoy experimenting	have the courage of their convictions	challenge the status quo
9. Discoveries depend on	being committed	being curious	being open-minded	having a broad perspective
10. A good writer	is convincing	presents new ideas	provides a unique perspective	has a compelling vision
11. Breakthrough thinking	makes progress possible	helps to solve difficult problems	explores new frontiers	encourages teamwork
12. I dislike	losing control	boring work	following rules	being rejected

TABLE 2-2 Creative Potential Profile, Version 5.1. (Continued)

13. I communicate best by being	direct	informative	interesting	open
14. I am committed to	achieving results	being the best at what I do	exploring new ideas	contributing to society
15. Creative organizations	look for good answers	encourage experimentation	allow freedom of expression	support new ideas
16. Achieving results depends on being	responsive	systematic	original	cooperative
17. I prefer situations where I	am in charge	have challenging assignments	can use my own ideas	can introduce change
18. Change depends on	gaining support	exploring options	independent thinking	inspiring others
19. My goal is to	accomplish my objectives	discover new approaches	have my ideas recognized	achieve progress
20. Leaders	assume responsibility	deal with complexity	visualize opportunities	empower others
21. Ethical behavior	is expected	requires honesty	emphasizes integrity	enhances society
22. The arts	help to improve designs	contribute new perspectives	broaden education	enrich people's lives
23. Creative thinkers	accomplish important goals	make significant discoveries	have leaps of imagination	turn their dreams into reality
24. Breaking with tradition	is seldom desirable	needs to be done carefully	provides new opportunities	helps to accomplish goals
25. When under pressure, I	trust my instincts	rely on known approaches	carefully explore my options	avoid conflict

The initial scores for the test instrument were derived from testing a number of individuals who were considered creative. These individuals were engaged in different kinds of work, covering a number of fields. These initial scores became the benchmark for determining the scores for each of the four styles. Following the initial research and changes in the test instrument, the average scores for each style were—

• Intuitive: 64

• Innovative: 67

• Imaginative: 58

• Inspirational: 61

The standard deviation for each of these categories was: 8, 7, 6, 6.

With these two sets of data, you can determine how you compare with a large number of individuals who have taken the Creativity Potential Profile. It is important to note, that scores which are "lower" than the average indicate a stronger emphasis in that category. The number 1 is considered the highest preference for a given category. The least desirable would be the number 4. Thus, a score that is higher than the average means it is less desirable. While this may be somewhat confusing, just remember that the lower the score the more you prefer a given category. If the average for Innovative, as shown above is 67 and your score was 57 this means that you have a higher than average preference for using the Innovative style. Remember, less is better! Results to date show that the scores are consistent regardless of one's background.

There is a relation between an individual's occupation and the scores. Thus, occupations that require action and results would tend to have lower scores (more 1's and 2's) for the Intuitive style, whereas, people involved in science or engineering would have lower scores for the Innovative category. The scoring was designed to measure an individual's preference for each creativity style rather than for a specific occupation.

Creative Intelligence reflects the complexity of humans and provides a description of a person's creativity. Most individuals have multiple styles of **Creative Intelligence**. As mentioned earlier, Michelangelo was an artist, sculptor, engineer, and scientist who fit three of the four categories of creativity (innovative, imaginative, and intuitive). In addition, we use each of the four styles differently. When one style is used frequently, this is called the most frequently used level of intensity. Just as there are four basic styles, each style can have four levels of intensity ranging from least used to most often used. The combination of each style with a level of intensity provides style "patterns." These patterns increase the possible types of creativity from 4 basic types to 256 creativity patterns. A sample computer-generated profile is shown in Figure 2–1.

Two important questions arise when considering Creative Intelligence styles. First, is there one best style? And second, how flexible can a person be? The conclusion is that there is no one best style. Rather, it depends on a style's appropriateness for a situation. In gen-

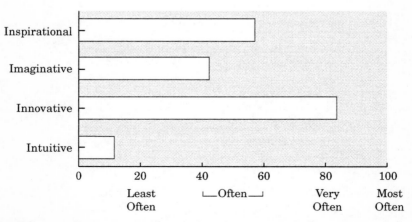

FIGURE 2-1 • Sample Creative Potential Profile test results.

eral, the extremes of being too flexible or too rigid are least effective. Rather than a single best style, a moderately flexible style appears more appropriate for most situations.

Personality Traits

Personality traits are descriptions of our behavior that reflect our values and beliefs. In turn, personality is reinforced by our genetic makeup and influences during early childhood. The importance of personality traits is that they have been used to describe expected behavior in many situations and are valid for predicting how Creative Intelligence will be used. Dacey and Lennon found that traits are important in relating personality to creativity. They studied traits such as having a high tolerance for ambiguity, being open-minded, and being at ease when faced with uncertainty or complexity. Their research helps to support the applicability of traits to determining a person's Creative Intelligence.

Genes and Their Relation to Behavior

An interesting study of traits was done by molecular biologist Dean Hamer. He found that genes were tied to personality. He and his colleagues at the National Institute of Health identified a gene on chromosome 11 that seemed to be linked to the trait called "novelty seeking," and another on chromosome 17 that may play a role in regulating anxiety. He didn't consider these genes to be the direct basis for behavior, but rather, he thought they were likely to contribute to the overall effect. Studying genes can be very difficult because DNA is made up of just four chemicals— adenine, guanine, cytosine, and thymine—but when taken together, they result in about a million combinations for any single human gene. Hamer also studied how different chemicals such as dopamine and serotonin affected the workings of the brain and regulated a person's moods. These chemicals are critical for understanding creativity because they affect reasoning, judgment, memory, and how we use our creativity.

An example where personality traits were used was for the Decision Style Inventory an earlier test by the author at the U.S. Post Office. The Post Office wanted to train 20 employees for the position of Postmaster at various locations in the U.S. They selected 110 individuals who were considered qualified for further training. All candidates endured 40 hours of intensive interviews, exercises, testing, and other approaches. The Post Office then selected 20 candidates. The Decision Style Inventory, based only on the use of traits and the scores for each style specified for the position, selected 19 of the 20 candidates.

At Union Bank of California, the Decision Style Inventory identified 19 of 20 top loan brokers. At Merrill-Lynch, it identified the top 36 out of 38 salespeople. All three of these cases had a 95% predictive accuracy. Can a test based on personality traits consistently achieve this level of predictability? Probably not, because it depends on the situation and on correctly identifying what traits are needed for success in a given occupation. However, in most cases, the use of test instruments such as the Decision Style Inventory or Creative Potential Profile are extraordinarily helpful and can avoid catastrophic choices. In one case, a newly hired Executive Vice President was not given any test. He was fired the following year at a cost approaching one million dollars, whereas the cost of the test would have been trivial. The old saying of being penny-wise and pound-foolish applies here.

What Leads to Creativity?

Where we have the freedom to explore new ideas or are willing to bend the rules, we can often expect creative results. **Creative individuals are able to grasp a situation in its entirety and are open to new pos-**

sibilities. They also have the courage of their convictions, are willing to risk failure, and are willing to wait for long periods before being rewarded for their accomplishments. They are very persistent and are willing to continue working for long periods of time despite obstacles and resistance.

Annette Moser-Wellman described *The Five Faces of Genius* as a way to help managers understand creative styles. Her hope was that this approach would go a long way toward a better understanding of how managers think. Working with Coca-Cola, her objective was to make changes in its corporate culture that would help the company learn how to foster innovation. She believed that creative and artistic people were rarely given the opportunity by their organzations to utilize their talents at work.

A question often raised is: Can we identify creative geniuses? The answer is that they are not mysterious individuals who pluck ideas out of thin air. They generally are people who work hard and rely on extensive research for their answers after studying many ideas. They also are flexible and are willing to go beyond standard approaches to find new answers and generate many ideas. Most of them keep accurate records of their progress and then elaborate and improve on their ideas. They incubate their ideas for long periods of time, which allows the subconscious to process unrelated factors to be incorporated into their thinking based on their Creative Intelligence.

Applying the Creative Potential Profile

Based on the studies that have been done, the Creative Potential Profile can be considered a sound basis for determining Creative Intelligence styles and for predicting an individual's creative behavior. The test instrument can also provide valuable support for teachers, managers, and all persons concerned with assuring that individuals who are creative are given appropriate support and are able to exercise their innate abilities.

Because the Creative Potential Profile is a valid test instrument, you can feel comfortable using it to determine your Creative Intelligence style. Furthermore, because of the ease of application, the instrument can be applied to many situations. The majority of people who have taken the test felt that it did measure their creative potential.

This is an opportunity waiting to be used. Considering the success of the Decision Style Inventory and the results to date, the Creative Potential Profile should have comparable results. If we support those with appropriate Creative Intelligence to utilize their abilities, we can solve difficult problems and come up with useful new inventions or ideas that have value for all of us. The buzzword in industry today is the desperate need for "innovation." With the rapid advance in technology and global competition, creativity is no longer a luxury. To survive, industry will have to utilize this valuable asset to achieve its goals.

Imagine what can be accomplished if we utilize this instrument to identify truly creative individuals. On the individual level, it would lead to a more satisfactory career. On a group level, it has the potential to release hidden potential and provide the basis for supporting those who have the ability to create. Too often, when it is not used, it leads to the loss of talented individuals and the contributions they could have made. It is no longer a matter of choice. Industry, education, government, and any organization that expects to survive in today's cutthroat environment will have to increasingly rely on creative individuals in the organization to lead the way to change.

3

WHAT CAN WE LEARN FROM CREATIVE INDIVIDUALS?

Those who dare to dream will find new worlds to conquer.

Those Who Create

Have you ever wondered how the lives of well-known individuals differ from the rest of the population? Can we gain insight into the nature of creativity by studying famous individuals and their creative accomplishments? Many people make significant contributions during their lives, but few achieve fame or recognition. However, the lives of well-known individuals can provide insight into our own creative potential.

Talent, ability, and knowledge are not the only ingredients needed to be creative. Creativity, in many respects, is like a living organism. It needs nourishment and support to achieve its full potential. Many famous individuals have achieved greatness, but it often took a toll on their personal lives. Einstein made incredible contributions to our understanding of the universe even though he was dyslexic, and his personal life was often in disarray. **Creative people have a burning passion that drives them to accomplish the impossible.**

Some derive their passion based on spirituality or a belief that is so strong it overrides all other considerations. Do all individuals believe that strongly in what they do?

Emma Policastro and Howard Gardner spent considerable time and effort researching the common factors and characteristics that influence creative productivity. They studied creative individuals in the arts and sciences and concluded that a *creative individual* is someone whose work had an impact in a specific area that was significant enough to influence future work in that area. Furthermore, they found that creative individuals generated many novel ideas. A hallmark of their study was that creative individuals were totally immersed in and obsessed with what they were doing. Their level of involvement often precluded close personal relationships and family life. Another finding was that **highly creative individuals carry their ideas with them all the time**. Gandhi and Freud, despite being married and having children, each chose celibacy relatively early in life to channel all their energies into their work. In Gardner's view, these were Faustian bargains that they hoped would allow them to make the most of their intellectual gifts. Creative individuals, such as entrepreneurs and inventors, also put their total energy into their work at the expense of having well-rounded lives.

Creative output depends on an individual's Creative Intelligence. In addition, creative people generally need knowledge about the field in which they hope to work. However, gaining knowledge can take many years of study to attain a thorough understanding, and **specialized training is often needed to achieve a high level of proficiency.** Madame Curie was a scientist long before she discovered X-rays.

Interestingly, individuals skilled in one field often contribute to related fields. Michelangelo was an artist, sculptor, *and* engineer. Experts, on the other hand, tend to rely on conventional practices within their own fields. In contrast, **many creative individuals question, explore outside their areas of expertise, and are willing to change their ideas**. They rely on imagination, in addition to knowledge within a given field, and go beyond what is normally expected of them. Those who blindly follow rules in any given field may be good problem-solvers, but they are not necessarily creative. These individuals can anticipate the nature of the final product they expect to achieve when they start their work. Building on their general knowledge, they focus on specific outcomes as work progresses.

You might wonder whether creative people knowingly deviate from societal norms. Their need for concentration, and their peculiar behavior, have led some people to question their mental stability. Their willingness to endure censure, however, can be a source of strength. Creative individuals focus on their abilities and ignore their weaknesses. **The truly creative individual willingly accepts failure as part of achieving results.** Thomas Edison, with virtually no formal education, hired the best scientists and engineers he could find to carry out his ideas. He considered the process of invention an art, and never stopped producing, undeterred by failures or the opinions of others.

Leonardo da Vinci painted the Mona Lisa and was also a sculptor, architect, engineer, and scientist. He focused on process, not the final product, often leaving work unfinished. With his scientific bent, he used systematic observation and analyzed details to understand the totality of the problem on which he was working. He constantly looked for key relationships and driving principles using diagrams, drawings, and graphs to formulate and solve problems. Interestingly, he produced thousands of notebook pages that provide a detailed record of his thinking. He believed that the best way to understand something was to study the details that make up the whole, moving from detail to detail. His mind had an incredible reach of curiosity.

One of da Vinci's techniques was to force a connection between two or more unrelated ideas. He discovered what came to be called the "Law of Continuity," finding that if the human brain deliberately concentrated on separate ideas or objects, it would eventually find a connection between them. He felt that the eye was the window to the soul, which led to an understanding and appreciation of the infinite works of nature. He felt that judgment led to errors where one assumed that results achieved were solely based on his or her experiments. Are there people today who are comparable to da Vinci? It would be difficult to find someone as versatile and outstanding in a number of different fields. Nonetheless, we can learn much about the creative mind by observing how creative individuals carried out their activities.

How to Enhance Creativity

Creative individuals respond to challenging goals and have confidence in what they are doing. When others provide them with reinforcement, it builds the creative person's confidence and helps motivate him or her. We often hear that creative people are nonconformists. In some cases, nonconformity can be a problem. For example, an airline pilot who does not follow rules could wreak havoc at an airport. The conflict between intellectual independence and disregard for authority needs to be considered. Out-of-control impulsiveness is generally not desirable.

A challenge facing educators, managers, and others in responsible positions is to find a balance between structure and freedom. They need to encourage creative expression and ensure freedom from ridicule or censure. In many cases, discipline, self-restraint, and respect for tradition and authority are just as important as freedom, spontaneity, innovativeness, and risk-taking. Ideally, you need a framework for creative expression without inhibiting it. An individual who is self-motivated and committed to what he or she is doing has great potential. Motivated individuals work to master the necessary knowledge to pursue their goals, in contrast to people who have considerable knowledge, but are not motivated to pursue new or challenging opportunities.

Creative individuals are driven by internal motivation, a passion to create, and in some cases, a belief that it is their divine duty to achieve specific goals rather than externally imposed goals. They tend to be unconventional, unconcerned with authority, and willing to take personal risks. Nonetheless, encouraging creativity can be challenging for anyone who manages such individuals. Teachers, trying to convey knowledge, often find precocious students difficult to deal with. The late physics professor Richard Feynman introduced a novel approach in his classroom. If the students didn't understand or follow what he was saying, they had a "red" flag that they could raise. Although sometimes this could be embarrassing, Feynman found that the approach created a sense of belonging by the students and had a positive learning effect.

People can be taught to think in new ways by following a number of simple approaches. The first is a willingness to compromise. The second is to change the approach taken to solving a problem. The third is to always consider another person's point of view. The following examples describe these three approaches:

- **Be willing to compromise**—When faced with a difficult situation, you cannot always achieve exactly what you want. Or, put another way, half a loaf is better than none. A case in point is the situation faced by a salesperson who insisted on full price and thus lost the customer. Then there is the situation where an individual wants a certain salary rather than an interesting occupation. We all make decisions that have pro's and con's. How we view a problem is based on our personality and values. What is right for you may not be the best for someone else. The willingness to compromise is often the secret to success.

- **Change the approach**—Edison hired a new engineer and asked him to find the amount of liquid needed to fill a light bulb. Using calculus, the engineer worked several hours and reported that it would require 23.3 cubic centimeters. Edison, who was somewhat absent-minded, asked what the measurement was for. The engineer reminded him of the assignment he had been given. Edison took the bulb and filled it with water. He then poured the water into a measuring cylinder and remarked that the engineer's result was "pretty close!"

- **Think of the opposite approach to doing things**—An example of this approach is the child who cried for new shoes until the parent pointed to the man who had no feet. If you put yourself in someone else's position, the change in perspective often leads to a meaningful response. Before criticizing someone, think about how you would feel if you were that person.

There are many creative ways to look at a problem rather than using an analytical approach. Finding new ways of looking at problems and finding answers is what distinguishes the truly creative person from someone who ignores the many possibilities that exist. Leonardo da Vinci would explore all possibilities and then document them. Look at what he accomplished!

Exploring the Creative Process

Me & Isaac Newton was a film documentary produced by Michael Apted at the University of Southern California. It examined the creative process by studying a number of scientists. People included in the documentary were:

- **Gertrude Elion**, a chemist, who won a Nobel Prize for the development of a drug to treat acute leukemia. Elion demonstrated a combination of the innovative and intuitive styles of Creative Intelligence.

- **Patricia Wright**, a primatologist, who discovered a new species of Malagasy lemur. She became interested in science only after buying a monkey at a New York pet shop. She exhibited a combination of the inspirational and innovative styles.

- **Ashok Gadgil**, an environmental scientist, who developed a cheap, practical method of water purification that is now widely used in developing nations. Here was an individual who used a combination of the innovative and intuitive styles.

- **Maja Mataric**, a computer scientist, who studied artificial intelligence and worked on research that led to the Sojourner robot, sent to Mars in 1997. Mataric was an example of combining the innovative and imaginative styles.

A significant finding from this study was that science and art are much more closely related than they appear at first. After considerable hard, methodical work, a point is reached where having faith helps one to take the great leap into the unknown that leads to a creative outcome. **Those willing to leap into the unknown may be surprised to find that they really were more creative than they had believed. They may even discover their hidden talent.**

Richard Feynman was more than just a great physicist. He was also a great educator, family man, and artist. With his wacky sense of humor and passion for teaching, he helped many non-scientists understand the basic concepts of physics. Twice in his life, he was honored by appointment to prestigious scientific organizations. In high school, he was inducted into Arista, and later into the National Academy of Science. Both organizations seemed to him to be more concerned with judging who was prestigious enough to belong rather than with promoting science. Consequently, he resigned from the National Academy of Science. As a teacher, he took great pride in having top scores from student evaluations. As a scientist winning the Nobel Prize (along with Shin'ichiro Tomanaga) for quantum electrodynamics, he said that the real prize was the pleasure of the discovery itself and seeing its usefulness. He undoubtedly was a combination of the innovative, imaginative, and inspirational styles.

Michael Michalko, in his book *Cracking Creativity*, describes creative-thinking strategies used by creative individuals and suggests that people in general can think creatively if they choose to do so.

Nobel Prize Winners

"The world's best minds can't—or won't—predict who might win a Nobel Prize." Nobel Prizes are given for outstanding achievement in physics, chemistry, medicine, literature, peace, and economics. Note that art, music, mathematics, engineering, computers, and other fields that make significant contributions are not included. In part, the omission of some fields of study was based on Alfred Nobel's objective of finding the best work that benefited mankind and world peace. Nobel is thought to have endowed the prizes to compensate for the destruction caused by the dynamite he invented. He conceived of dynamite as a peacetime tool to solve problems such as digging the Panama Canal.

Starting in 1901, there have been 112 prizes in physics, 89 in chemistry, 54 in literature, 47 for peace effort, and 49 in economics. Some recent winners include Richard Feynman in quantum electrodynamics, Barry Sharpless for asymmetric epoxidation, Stanley Prusiner for the discovery of prions, John Steinbeck for the book *Of Mice and Men*, Herbert Abrams for ways to prevent nuclear war, and Harry Markowitz for the Portfolio Theory.

In 2001, the Nobel Foundation celebrated its first 100 years with a centennial exhibition of the Nobel Peace Prize. The exhibition and a companion book, *Cultures of Creativity*, explored the creative process of individuals and how the environment can foster creativity for the benefit of mankind. The exhibition celebrated key characteristics of creative individuals, including the "courage to think on entirely new lines, daring to question established theories," and "innovative combinations of insights from different fields."

The current interest in creativity has generated a major project called the *Encyclopedia of Creativity*. Some of the topics to be covered include the following: Adaptation and Creativity, Cognitive Style and Creativity, Creativity in the Future, Enhancement of Creativity, Giftedness and Creativity, Perception and Creativity, and Teaching Creativity.

Even though there is no specific Nobel Prize for "creativity," it is interesting to note the level of effort being expended in studying various aspects of the field.

What Is Different About Creative Individuals?

Comparing the lives and works of well-known individuals reveals a number of interesting findings. For instance, what did Hans Christian Anderson, Alexander Graham Bell, George Burns, Winston Churchill, Leonardo da Vinci, Walt Disney, Thomas Edison, Albert Einstein, Henry Ford, General George S. Patton, and Jack Welch have in common? All were dyslexic. Dyslexia is a condition in which written letters and numbers are perceived backwards. This can result in patterns that are confusing. In spite of this disability, all of these individuals found ways to learn and became outstanding achievers. Lincoln, Churchill, and others who were largely self-educated went on to become highly successful leaders. In the creative style categories, Lincoln was a high inspirational, a high imaginative, and a strong innovative. Think of the Gettysburg Address and the Lincoln-Douglas debates. Lincoln's major shortcoming was his low level of the intuitive style. His generals during the Civil War constantly complained that Lincoln would tell them not to kill people, if possible. What an incredible individual! He was able to visualize what it took to be a strong nation.

Artists such as da Vinci, Picasso, Rembrandt, and Van Gogh were all highly productive and had their own unique ways of viewing the world around them. They were all highly imaginative and strongly intuitive. Beethoven, Mozart, and Stravinsky were prolific composers and excellent pianists who also were highly imaginative and intuitive. Each was able to visualize entire compositions and was able to produce magnificent work. Outstanding educators such as Forman, Griffin, and Whirry, all recent winners of the National Teacher of the Year Award, love learning and believe passionately in people. They are highly inspirational and intuitive. Their love for learning has led them to dedicating their lives to teaching.

Inventors have attributes that help them achieve outstanding results. Edison, Ford, Carrier, DuPont, and Stradivarius all were able to extend current knowledge to achieve significant new results. Each made contributions that are still used to this day. They were all highly innovative and intuitive thinkers. Stradivarius produced stringed instruments that still have not been surpassed. Brilliant tones emanate from the violins of Antonio Stradivarius, crafted in the 17th and 18th Centuries. These tones have baffled researchers for years. Joseph Nagyvary of Texas A&M University, however, claims that the secret lies in the chemistry of the construction materials.

Generally leaders are not thought of in terms of creativity. Yet, people such as Churchill, Eisenhower, and Benjamin Franklin each demonstrated an outstanding ability to inspire and influence people during times of crisis. They each inspired confidence and overcame difficult situations by using their sharp minds, having a willingness to take risks, and demonstrating a passionate desire to accomplish their goals. They had a combination of the inspirational, imaginative, and intuitive Creative Intelligence styles.

Individuals such as Gandhi, King, Nightingale, Eleanor Roosevelt, and Mother Teresa worked tirelessly to bring about significant change in people's lives. They too were inspirational and intuitive.

Kelleher at Southwest Airlines, Jack Welch at GE, and others have excelled in accomplishing the seemingly impossible task of growing their companies beyond expectation. They were a combination of the innovative and intuitive styles. Each focused intensely on specific goals, firm in the belief that they had a mission to accomplish—the goals they had set out to achieve. Without goals and being driven by a passionate desire to excel, we would not have many of the wonders of the world we currently enjoy.

Medicine has seen extraordinary advances in recent years because of people such as DeBakey and Salk. Along with medical missionaries such as Albert Schweitzer, they laid the foundation for improving life by their willingness to make personal sacrifices. Medical researchers in the fields of biotechnology and genetics and inventors of devices such as magnetic resonant imaging (MRI) continue to enhance our ability to live longer and healthier lives because of their dedication, sacrifice, and a strong belief in what they are doing. These individuals exhibit a combination of the innovative and inspirational styles.

Scientists have had a profound influence on the world. Darwin, Curie, and Freud each laid foundations that broke new ground in controversial fields. They persevered in the face of opposition and immersed themselves in their work, often at the cost of great personal sacrifice. They were highly innovative and inspirational.

Artists, writers, and poets have enriched society and culture throughout human history. Often, individuals in this category exhibit a combination of the imaginative, intuitive, and inspirational styles to help shape the minds of the world. Shakespeare, Dickens, and Clemens have still to be equaled. They were each able to express universal truths about everyday experience by creating fictional worlds that transfixed audiences and readers and have endured over time. Thoreau, Whitman, Woolf, and Welty were able to observe people and relate behavior to universally appreciated beauty in the words they wrote. Most creative people use their remarkable insight to create work that persists long after their own lives.Scientists who look at problems from new perspectives are able to introduce concepts and approaches that have a universal impact. Galileo, Newton, Einstein, and Feynman are among those who have achieved results that changed our perception of reality. They were a combination of the high innovative and high imaginative styles.

Neurologist Semir Zeki believes that the production of art and the function of the visual brain are similar. He describes the outline of a biologically based theory of aesthetics. It may seem difficult to understand how visualization depends on the aesthetic experience that can produce a work of art, or the neurology of the accompanying emotional experience. However, while there are inherent limitations in a neurological basis for aesthetics, Zeki describes in his book, *Inner Vision*, the foundation of neuro-aesthetics, in an attempt to better understand the biological basis of aesthetic experience. Zeki points out that there is a universality of emotional or aesthetic response relating Shakespeare, Wagner, and Beethoven. He attributes a profound understanding of human reaction to these creative giants. Perhaps it was their common level of Creative Intelligence.

Each creative individual discussed in this chapter, in his or her way, made a major contribution stemming from ability, uniqueness, and a willingness to endure self-sacrifice, along with the feeling that he or she had a mission to carry out. Almost universally, each had an overwhelming desire to achieve what seemed unattainable. They often had to deal with "conventional wisdom," which would have daunted most people and prevented human progress. Instead, they went against the crowd to achieve extraordinary results.

There have also been remarkable families throughout history who have had multiple achievers over generations. The Bach family of 17th Century Germany produced talented musicians and composers. In the visual arts, there were the Renoirs, Breugels, and Wyeths. Generations of British actors came from the Barrymore family. Scientists are studying this phenomenon and trying to discover the balance between genes and environment. One study by University of California at Davis psychologist Dean Keith Simonton suggests that gifted parents who had children when they themselves were young had more of an influence over those children than parents who waited until they were older and more established.

Creativity Is Not Affected by Age

Wayne Dennis studied the lives of 738 creative scientists and demonstrated that age does not inhibit creativity. Based on his research, scholars and artists (mostly men) who lived to be at least 79 were still creative. He explored patterns of productivity throughout careers of individuals, decade by decade. Scholars and scientists were least productive in their twenties, and most productive during their forties, fifties, and sixties. Most continued to be productive well into their seventies, at which point productivity dropped back to the levels of their twenties. The productivity of artists tended to peak in their forties, and they, too, remained productive into their sixties and seventies at rates similar to those in their twenties.

Dennis suggested that youthful vigor did not seem to play a major role in creativity. He attributed differences to the fact that for scholars and scientists, there is a longer period required to become proficient in knowledge about a given domain. Artists depend primarily on their creative imagination. Their performance peaked earlier in their career and then fell off sharply in later years. Scholars and scientists often are able to hire assistants to support their efforts into their later years.

Gerontologist/psychiatrist Gene D. Cohen takes issue with the common assumption that creative potential dwindles with age, and also that it is limited to gifted individuals. People need to understand that creativity continues to be possible and can be enhanced by the empowering effect of continued creative activity. There are many examples of creative productivity by individuals well beyond "retirement" age. Cohen describes creative potential in later life as depending on the knowledge accumulated along with the individual's psychological/emotional growth and wisdom. He cites examples of famous individuals who were creative well into old age. Michelangelo, who had an imaginative/innovative style, worked on the architectural design for the dome of St. Peter's Basilica from age 72 to 88; Sarah Bernhardt, who had an imaginative/intuitive style, lost a leg in her early 70s, but continued to perform on stage until her death at age 78; Frank Lloyd Wright, who had an imaginative/innovative style, completed his design of New York's Guggenheim Museum at age 91; and Agatha Christie, who had an imaginative/intuitive style, oversaw production of the film *Murder on the Orient Express* at age 84. We are better able to appreciate our gift of creative talent when we observe the accomplishments of others. These examples clearly demonstrate that people can stay creative well into old age.

Paul McCartney described the creative process of the Beatles as spontaneous; they often had no idea what they'd be doing and would record without rehearsals. In her early years as a journalist, Isabel Allende was able to write anywhere, the kitchen counter, a closet, a car. Now she wants silence and solitude, and has a room of her own. Her definition of creativity includes every aspect of life, from finding unusual uses for ordinary household appliances to making her own clothes. She feels that's what creativity is; it's not always something to do with the arts or writing. It has to do with the way you carry out your life.

Maxine Hong Kingston, at age 59, describes her parents as being creative and active until their deaths at 100 and 90+. She claims to have more productive energy in mid-life than ever before. She feels that she is much more effective than when she was young. She lost her last book-in-progress in a fire that destroyed her home. It took her eight more years and a lot of determination to complete it. Gore Vidal, at age 74, writes shortly after he wakes up. This keeps him closest to the dream world. Vidal believes that living life intensely is a prerequisite to writing well. He goes to Italy to be alone to write, and returns to Los Angeles to experience life.

The capacity to learn extends far beyond the early years. An individual's brain activity facilitates more brain activity, responding to challenges both physically and chemically. Stimulation of the brain promotes growth of new connections to various parts of the brain. Under the right circumstances, some individuals are able to find new ideas that cover an entire field. Others, such as retired attorney Jason Riley, took on a case (as a volunteer) at age 85 and saved a local community center that was destined for commercial use.

What Can We Learn from These Outstanding Individuals?

How can you use the information about creative people to change your life? First, you need to know your preferred Creative Intelligence styles. If you match your styles with what has been described about creative people, you can decide whether you want to pursue a given field. Considerable evidence is available that shows we can achieve greater satisfaction when we are doing what "comes naturally." Given that starting point, one could, for example, go to art school or take more advanced courses in specific fields. Often we hear someone say, "I could never do that," when they have never really tried. We need to recognize that almost every famous person spent many hours practicing and studying in a given field. The expression "Greatness is the result of dedication and perspiration" fits almost every creative person.

Each of the individuals discussed in this chapter had an extraordinary effect on the world, either directly or indirectly. Can you, in turn, apply these findings to your life? Yes, if you have the courage to pursue activities that on the surface appear too difficult. Some people consider the impossible a challenge, and unlike "the man from La Mancha," they do achieve the impossible dream. **You need to have the courage of your convictions and be willing to pursue difficult goals even under adverse conditions**. This dedication does not come without pain, but the satisfaction is well worth the effort. Lincoln had no formal education; he was selected to run for the presidency because he was a dark horse. Yet, we still admire his many contributions and his staunch belief that a nation divided would not survive.

A Sampling of Creative Individuals

Below are details about the lives of four well-known individuals. They each pursued different occupations, yet in their own way, made significant contributions to our society.

Katherine Hepburn

Katherine Hepburn was born in 1907 and lived to 2003. She won four Academy Awards for acting. One of her strengths was that she exhaustively researched and prepared for roles. She focused on her career and was very ambitious. Early in life, she knew that she wanted to become an actress. While greatly loved by the movie-going public, she remained aloof from her peers throughout her long career. Notoriously self-centered, she focused almost exclusively on acting and stayed away from most social activities. A hard worker, she prepared for roles with meticulous research and was known for her flawless ability to memorize her lines. Fiercely independent, Hepburn managed her career with as much care as she did acting itself, carefully cultivating her aristocratic image. She used money and influence to get roles that would exploit her strengths, and she went out of her way to avoid productions that she believed would harm her image. She epitomizes the intuitive and imaginative style of Creative Intelligence.

Rembrandt van Rijn

Rembrandt van Rijn lived from 1606 to 1669. He is undoubtedly one of the most famous artists who lived. His ability to master light and shadow demonstrated a deep insight into portraying human nature. He was systematic in his study of portraiture and was highly productive. He endured the deaths of four children, his wife, and then his second wife. Interestingly, his greatest works were produced late in life. His drawings and etchings reflect his masterful skill as an artist. Although his parents were of modest means, they provided him with an excellent education.

He left school as a teenager to study painting under a local master. He made rapid progress and moved to Amsterdam, where he worked with another famous master. By the age of 22, he had students of his own and shortly becoming famous. Rembrandt produced hundreds of drawings and etchings along with many paintings, including over 60 self-portraits. He too exhibited the combination of intuitive and imagintive styles.

Jean Piaget

Jean Piaget, 1896–1980, was a scientist and philosopher who profoundly influenced early-childhood education by being a keen observer of children's behavior. He developed some very important insights into how children think and recognized the importance of discovery in the learning process. Piaget recognized that children think differently than adults; they have their own special kind of logic. Children, he believed, were not "empty vessels" to be filled with knowledge by means of education. He suggested that children were in fact little scientists who were constantly testing their own theories of how the world worked. The implications of Piaget's theory were enormous for education. He studied the reasoning processes of children and came to believe that understanding how children's minds worked was the key to understanding human knowledge.

While not an educator, Piaget had a profound impact on education. He emphasized the use of discovery as the best means for learning. His approach was not to *tell* children about the world. He maintained that children best understood what they themselves invented. He demonstrated a combination of innovative and imaginative styles.

William Shakespeare

Shakespeare lived from 1564 to 1616. He was a playwright and poet who wrote in iambic pentameter, which has inspired people for 400

years. He demonstrated remarkable insight into human nature and created universal characters and plots in his writings. His most famous
plays include *Hamlet, Romeo and Juliet,* and *King Lear.*

Shakespeare is generally considered one of the greatest dramatists
and poets the world has ever known. He had remarkable insight into
human nature, using universal human qualities to create highly individual characters that were easily recognizable. Shakespeare had a broad
knowledge of many subjects, including music, law, the stage, politics,
and history. His contributions to the English language are hard to over-
estimate; his plays have long been a required part of Western education. His ideas on romantic love, heroism, comedy, and tragedy have
influenced millions of people. His words still hold magic for audiences
around the world.

Shakespeare's collected plays were published seven years after his
death in a large, expensive volume called the *First Folio.* He is thought
to be the most quoted writer in the world. In expressing deep thoughts
and feeling, he used words of great power and beauty. His technical
skills as a poet were highly developed; he was a master of rhythm,
sound, image, and metaphor. His range included the grandly formal
speech of the nobility and the earthy puns of the common people. He
had a combination intuitive, innovative, and imaginative styles.

What Have We Learned?

Having explored the lives of famous and well-known people from
a diverse universe, the question is: What can we learn about creativity
from reading this material? An objective review of this diverse group
shows there is considerable commonality among these individuals.
They were all high achievers who dedicated their lives to accomplishing something of value, and that has had enduring benefit to mankind.

By reviewing the lives of creative people, you can gain a perspective that helps to explain what it takes to be a contributor to a given

field. The conclusion is obvious: If you are not creating, you are missing out on life! **For those who have a desire for greatness, creativity is the only game in town.**

The following summarizes how famous individuals utilized their Creative Intelligence:

- They used bold, frame-breaking thinking and had a willingness to deviate from accepted practices—Florence Nightingale changed hospital sanitation and pioneered practices used in modern nursing.

- They invented new approaches—De Bono introduced the concept of "lateral think," which differed from conventional approaches to problem solving that typically used logical or deductive reasoning.

- They had the courage of their convictions and were willing to take risks in the face of uncertainty—Galileo Galilei challenged the church's authority with his scientific theories. Churchill had a driving compulsion in his heroic leadership during World War II.

- They envisioned what could not be seen and thereby achieved "the impossible dream"—Chagall painted mystical scenes that reflected his spiritual convictions.

- They explored new or different approaches, or extended a given field—Igor Stravinsky changed classical music by introducing an entirely new approach.

- They willingly undertook challenging projects—Wolfgang Amadeus Mozart composed enduring music; Charles Darwin developed the Theory of Evolution.

- They persisted in their search for excellence and delved into the unknown to find gold in the haystack—Antonio Stradivarius' violins remain unsurpassed to this day. Michael DeBakey made significant medical discoveries and innovations.

- They constantly searched for alternatives— Jean Piaget's observations of children had a profound impact on modern education; Jonas Salk produced the first working polio vaccine.

- They had a willingness to question current approaches—Jaime Escalante encouraged extraordinary performance from disadvantaged students in the study of calculus.

- They were willing to try everything—Marie Curie discovered radium and polonium; Galileo invented the age of science with his experiments in astronomy.

- They had a positive self-image, perseverance, and curiosity— President Franklin D. Roosevelt led a nation in crisis; Katharine Hepburn exhaustively studied the characters she had to act.

- They overcame difficulties in the environment—Elaine Griffin customized curriculum for students in remote Alaskan schools who otherwise would not have had an education.

- They made things work under unusually difficult conditions— Katharine Graham led *The Washington Post* to greatness. She was an outstanding author who continued her work in the midst of an impeachment that changed the U.S. Presidency forever. Dwight Eisenhower led the Normandy invasion against great odds; Churchill kept a stiff upper lip under extremely harsh conditions.

Given ability, personality, drive, and a propensity for risk-taking, most people can make significant contributions. Can anyone become famous? Probably not, but many could do so if they recognized their potential. **The Creative Potential Profile can encourage you to assert yourself and accomplish what you never thought possible.**

4

USING OUR
CREATIVE ABILITY

Follow your dreams, for they give life a purpose.

Creative Problem-Solving

There is little doubt that some individuals are better at solving problems than others. Creative individuals enjoy a challenge and tend to look at problems as a means of achieving goals. Because individuals differ in their Creative Intelligence, they use different approaches to solving problems. Is there a best way to approach problem-solving? Obviously, the answer depends on the problem solver's Creative Intelligence style and the kind of problem one is facing.

Thus, creative problem-solving involves more than finding a good solution. **Problem-solving requires taking into account who is solving the problem, how it is solved, and how the solution is implemented. Finding a good solution is not enough.** In an organization, a solution must be introduced and accepted by the people responsible for the outcome. The organization must be open to new ideas and possible radical change. The level of commitment made, the motivation of those involved in finding a solution, and the expected satisfaction with the solution often determines its ultimate success. **Few solutions emerge unscathed from the complex realities within organizations. Simply put, you are not always able to foresee all the possible difficulties that might arise, or to know in advance how to deal with them when setting out to implement a solution.** A positive attitude and a sense of responsibility often determine the success of a proposed solution. In addition, involving those who will be implementing a solution, contributes to gaining acceptance.

How We See Problems

Our mental framework reflects our Creative Intelligence and determines how we see the world around us. How often do witnesses to a crime each report different things even though there is only one reality? *Frameworks*—the prisms through which we view the world—determine both what we see and how we interpret it. Frameworks also affect the decisions we make and our personal values determine what we prefer to do. Deeply held beliefs tend to persevere even when evidence shows them to be wrong. To circumvent this limitation, you would have to step out of the box and ask yourself, "Am I being reasonable?" By being open-minded, you can release your creative potential and the rewards will be well worth the effort.

It is virtually impossible to separate an individual's values from the judgments he or she makes. A problem that seems overwhelming to one person may be a stimulating challenge to another. A person who has had experience with a given situation will generally be more confident about finding a solution. **The willingness to take a risk, however, is what will determine whether or not an individual will attempt to solve a problem.**

Finding Solutions

Problem-solving seldom follows a simple path; rather, it is a difficult process that is impeded by politics, feelings, and so on. An example is the case of the president of a consulting firm who had a conflict with his executive vice president. It turned out that the president felt isolated because all the department heads reported directly to the executive vice president. A consultant who was called in to help with the problem started by interviewing the president, the executive vice president, and all the department heads. It was obvious that the real problem was a conflict of personalities. To find a solution to the problem, however, a creative approach was needed. The consultant held a number of meetings with the president to explore possible alternatives and suggested moving the executive vice president to another position in the company so that the department heads would then report directly to the president. But, how does one convince the executive vice president to move aside? The consultant had to find a way to resolve this dilemma. Not only would a creative solution be needed, but also, it had to be sold to all the parties involved. After considering many alternatives, the consultant came up with the idea of offering the executive vice president a position that matched his real interest.

Over a one-month period, group meetings were held with all the people involved to allow them to openly express their ideas. After these meetings and individual discussions, it was suggested that the executive vice president be assigned the role of "Director of Advanced Technology Development." The change would put him in direct contact with customers and would give him responsibility for introducing new technology into the firm. This change met the needs of the executive vice president, who enjoyed travel and utilizing his technical background. It also met the needs of the lonely president.

This example illustrates how complex a seemingly simple problem can be. A number of approaches were required to identify a solution, find a basis for acceptance, and implement the solution. The result was a resounding improvement in the functioning of the firm.

How Are Problems Defined?

Problems can be categorized in many ways. There are problems in which the cause appears to be known. Other problems are well-defined, but there are few alternatives, such as when a refrigerator won't work because it isn't plugged into an electrical outlet. Then, there are problems for which there is no obvious cause, where the answer is uncertain, and where there are many alternatives. **Complex problems generally involve a number of unknown factors. Problems that on the surface appear simple may in reality be very complex and have deeper underlying causes.** For example, when a person behaves in a seemingly "irrational" manner, there is almost always a reason for doing so. A case in point was the question of whether safety devices to prevent overhead cranes from hurting workers should be installed. The search was discontinued after two years on the claim that there were no funds available to install the new devices. In reality, the general manager had made up his mind at the very first meeting with the union, when he declared he was not certain that funds were available to make the changes suggested.

A Problem-Solving Example

On a cold and dreary November morning, the new Director of Research arrived for work at the Hughes Aircraft Company. Shortly after his arrival, he was summoned into the Vice President's office.

"Welcome to Hughes," the Vice President said. "We are canceling ADMA!"

Somewhat astounded, the new Director asked, "What is ADMA?" "It's that new automatic drafting machine," came the reply.

"But, why are you canceling the project?" the Director asked inno-
cently.

"Because I have never seen it work!" came the reply.

"How long do I have to make it work?" asked the Director. Somewhat amazed by the question, the Vice President said that he would need
an answer in four weeks as to whether to continue or cancel the project.

So started the first of many actions needed to develop a working
prototype of the automatic drafting machine, or ADMA. By the end of
the first four weeks, a new language had been developed that could
translate an engineer's sketch into a form that the computer could use
to drive the drafting machine. After seeing the ADMA perform, the
project was approved by the Vice President. However, many technical
problems had to be overcome along the way, including the development of the first daisy-wheel printer.

After the first year of operation, during which time the ADMA
produced computer-driven, inked 8-foot drawings, the Air Force
decided that what it really wanted were 16-foot drawings. Key project
members were hastily summoned for a Friday morning meeting. At
8:15 a.m., one of the programmers arrived, explaining that he had
stayed up until 3:00 a.m. working on the problem, without success. The
Director of Research had promised that the meeting would end at noon,
but as time passed, he realized there was no solution in sight. In desper-
ation, at 11:45, he suggested that the programmers make a modification
to the computer program so that when the program reached 8 feet, a
counter would be reset to zero that would restart the process. It worked
like a charm and saved the day! By applying a simple but creative
approach, a seemingly impossible problem was solved.

This example illustrates that **there are few problems that cannot
be solved given the right perspective and approach**. Examples
abound that demonstrate knowing what to do; anyone can be creative
by combining innate talent with tenacity and risk-taking. Consider that
at one time we believed the sun rotated around the earth. We now know

that the opposite is true. Who would have believed that humans could fly to the moon? Each time a discovery is made, whether it is X-rays, DNA, the polio vaccine, or computer chips, people wonder why things that seemed so obvious after the fact were so difficult to see the first time. Problem-solving is not just finding elegant solutions, but it involves using basic knowledge and being willing to accept new approaches to find workable solutions.

Where Does Creative Problem-Solving Start?

In most cases, creative problem-solving starts with having relevant expertise. In addition, creative solutions stem from each individual's unique Creative Intelligence. **Using rigid, inflexible approaches to solving problems can lead to seemingly good solutions that turn out, in practice, to be of little value.** Where there is little knowledge to build on at the start, one needs to rely on symptoms, clues, trends, or other relevant information. From the start, one needs to avoid jumping to conclusions. Think of the classic case of whether a glass is seen as half-full or half-empty. Obviously, while either is correct in describing the glass of liquid, the way it is viewed can lead to different conclusions and actions. British Airways always considers the glass "half-empty" and the flight attendants proceed to "fill it up." From a customer relations' perspective, this approach enhances a passenger's view of British Airways.

In some cases, it is not a simple matter to know if there is a problem. For instance, a movie theater had plastic covers on the stage lamps. The heat of one of the lamps caused a plastic cover to start smoldering. Seeing the smoke, the audience panicked, and many ran for the doors. A few people recognized that the immediate danger was not a small fire, but the likelihood of being trampled by the crowd. Those who correctly diagnosed the situation simply stayed in their seats, while some of those who rushed out were hurt by the crush of people trying to get out.

Creative problem-solving is often a matter of attitude, not the method or approach used. Consider the case of a student who moved to a new job in a different state before completing his master's degree. He requested permission from the school's associate dean to take his last two courses at a university in the city to which he had moved. Permission was granted, and the student completed the required two courses. When he applied for his degree, however, the registrar considered that one of the two courses was the equivalent of an undergraduate course. Based on this interpretation, the registrar refused to grant the degree. Compounding the problem, the associate dean who had originally granted permission was no longer at the university.

The new associate dean, when confronted with the problem of a highly agitated student, looked for a creative way to solve the problem. He felt that the student had completed the requirements for the degree. The question now was how to deal with the registrar who had rejected the student's request for the degree. After considerable discussion with the assistant dean, the new associate dean recommended that the student be given retroactive permission to take an undergraduate course. Using an approved undergraduate elective was allowed in the completion of a master's degree. Retroactive permission was granted, and the student received his degree. This approach avoided what might have been a difficult situation.

Before embarking on solving a problem, you need to decide whether or not it is worth solving the problem at all. There are times when resources, lack of knowledge, or lack of time do not permit finding a solution. **Problem-solving often involves reasoning along with creativity and depends on how an individual perceives the information that is available.** Even when a problem is clear, fixation and prejudice can prevent an individual from being willing to find a solution. The mind has only a limited view of a problem, and judgment is not always reliable for determining what to do. Unfortunately, judgment tends to be selective and supports existing beliefs. This is called the "primacy effect," which results in a biased interpretation of information, and often can be inappropriate for finding a good solution.

Approaches to Creative Problem-Solving

One approach to problem-solving that has proven extremely powerful is called *heuristics*. It has been used to help solve seemingly "unsolvable" problems. It is based on observation, experience, and Creative Intelligence. The word "heuristic" comes from the Greek *heuriskein*, which means to invent, or discover. **Heuristic thinking does not necessarily proceed in a direct manner. It involves searching, experimenting, evaluating, and reappraising all the available information as the processes of exploring and probing take place.** The knowledge gained from success or failure at various steps is taken into account and then used to further modify the process. More often than not, it is necessary to redefine either the desired objectives or the problem itself. Because heuristics are not based on formal logic, there is no simple or general rule to follow. Rather, heuristics involve the use of intuition, experience, and Creative Intelligence to explore various options.

Although heuristics provide a powerful approach to solving complex problems; a shortcoming to using heuristics is that the approach does not assure finding the "best" possible answer. Nonetheless, in almost every case, the use of heuristics does provide a very good answer. A significant advantage of using heuristics is that the approach can be readily understood by the user, and therefore it is more likely to be accepted and implemented.

An interesting case was the use of heuristics to find a solution to what is known as the "traveling salesman problem." This problem deals with the question of how to find the shortest distance one has to travel when visiting a large number of different locations. Interestingly, the following heuristic approach to the problem was reasonably straight-

FIGURE 4-1   The traveling salesman problem.

forward and did not require the use of computers or complicated formulas.

Figure 4–1 shows the problem confronting a person who has to
visit a large number of customers scattered across the U.S. To find the
shortest distance, the following heuristic rules apply:

1. Always travel along the exterior path.

2. Do not backtrack.

3. Do not make any crossovers.

This approach enables one to look ahead and visually determine
which direction to go based on the three rules above. The rules can be
restated as: Follow the outside path (never go to the inside); always
move forward and do not backtrack; and finally, do not crisscross the
path because that increases the distance traveled. Figure 4–2 is a sample solution for the salesperson who has to visit the locations shown in
Figure 4–1.

This solution was shown to the president of a company that deliv-
ered furniture to over 30 cities in the western part of the U.S. Because

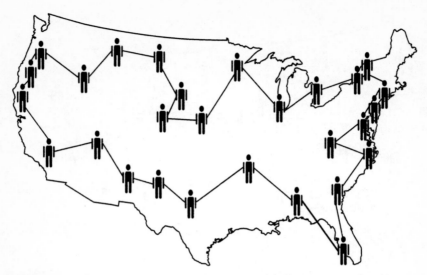

FIGURE 4-2   Heuristic solution to the traveling salesman problem.

there were both drop-offs and pick-ups of returns, the problem was difficult to visualize. However, using a map (such as the one shown
above) that clearly identified where the cities were located and using
the traveling salesman heuristic approach just described, it was simple
to find the shortest route that should be taken. The president was able to
readily visualize the solution, and easily followed the logic. He had no
difficulty in applying it to his business.

Heuristics rely on Creative Intelligence to finding solutions to
extremely complex problems. Early work in the field of heuristics dealt
with problems such as chess-playing and pattern recognition for the
military. In essence, the heuristic approach utilizes Creative Intelligence to arrive at non-mathematical solutions to complex problems.
The heuristic approach is easily understood by what one is doing. The
results belong to the user, and thus he/she feels more comfortable using
the approach. Heuristics have also been applied to problems involving
organizations, airline scheduling, and medical treatment, among others. Thus, in reality, heuristics provide a creative approach for dealing
with many of the problems that confront us.

Heuristics can even be used in explaining mathematical problems such as teaching calculus. A professor teaching an introductory course in business math struggled with the formulas needed to explain the fundamentals. Realizing that the class did not understand the material, the professor decided to try heuristics as a way of explaining the problem. After seeing the ease with which the material could be explained using a graphical approach rather than a mathematical approach, one of the students exclaimed, "Why wasn't this approach used rather than the mathematical one?" The student understood! How often are we trapped into using a formal approach to solving a problem rather than one that is intuitively obvious?

Another heuristic approach that has been used for many years is one that shows a small percentage of all problems account for the majority of the outcome. For example, a small percentage of all employees are the ones who are always late. **Managers have long known that a problem can always be separated into more important and less important parts.** For example, they know that a small percentage of customers contribute to most of the profit. This allows individuals to concentrate on the more important parts of a problem and save time and money. One example was a problem at a GE plant. Two consultants were trying to find a way to improve productivity and were stymied. They called headquarters for help. A member of the corporate staff explained that they needed to only look at the "important" part of the problem rather than all aspects. This solved the problem.

Edward DeBono, who has done extensive research on creative problem-solving, uses an approach called *lateral think*. This approach employs an open, or creative, approach to finding solutions rather than a logical approach. He used this to solve many problems that on the surface appeared too difficult to find an answer.

Insight, intuition, and creativity, when combined, generally offer a better solution than a deductive, logical approach. The reason is fairly straightforward. Most problems involve people. People respond better to solutions that consider how they think and behave rather than ones that only consider cost or timing.

Bob Hornby, a former Chairman of the Board of Southern California Gas, stated, "There are no problems at my company—only opportunities." What an incredible approach! He recognized that every problem also was an "opportunity" to do something different. His creativity made Southern California Gas a very profitable and well-run company.

Other Approaches to Creative Problem-Solving

Often, a solution to a problem turns out to be difficult because the problem has been viewed improperly. For example, consider the question of how to determine the best sequence of courses for an undergraduate curriculum. At one school, there were 5 courses for each of 8 semesters, or a total of 40 courses that needed to be scheduled. Viewed as possible combinations of 40 courses, the problem becomes "unmanageable." However, by recognizing that what we really have is 8 sets of 5 courses, the problem reduces to choosing which courses have prerequisites. Basic courses would be offered first, followed by a sequence that looks at requirements rather than considering all possible sequences of the 40 courses.

Another approach to problem-solving is the use of computers and artificial intelligence. The real potential of computers lies in the far-reaching implications for the ways in which problems can be solved. There is little doubt that computers can be made to behave in increasingly "intelligent" ways and are faster and more accurate than any human could ever be. However, a creative approach incorporates human "expertise" into computer programs. Nonetheless, artificial intelligence has become increasingly useful in many applications.

"Artificial intelligence," in some respects, is a misnomer. Computers may behave in intelligent ways, but by no means are they

creative, nor do they have the problem-solving ability of humans.
For example, Big Blue, IBM's chess program, did not really beat the
chess champion of the world. Rather, a clever programmer used rules
that the computer executed at superhuman speed to beat the champion.
Big Blue did not really have its own intelligence; rather, it demonstrated an intelligent application that depended on speed that was far
beyond a human's capability.

There are many ways in which computers can add to the human
ability to solve problems. For example, a computer program at Boston
University Hospital was used to determine how best to deliver chemo-
therapy to patients. Some of the protocols involved over 1,000 steps
that no human could remember while at the same time testing for the
toxicity of the medication. Physicians would not be capable of carrying
out certain procedures without the support of computers. Likewise, we
could not send humans to the moon without computer assistance.
Weather forecasting and the Internet depend on computers. An emerging field in education is computer-assisted distance learning. Even
remote surgery depends on computer displays in distant locations to
assist doctors in carrying out complex procedures that otherwise could
not be undertaken.

An interesting use of artificial intelligence was a program called
"Cooker," which was developed to automatically diagnose and maintain
the huge cooking kettles for Campbell's Soup. The chief engineer had
reached the age of 65 and was ready to retire, and no one else had the
experience or knowledge to maintain and repair the huge kettles, despite
some very creative approaches. An engineer who was an expert in finding the rules used to maintain the huge kettles was hired to identify and
document the approach used by Campbell's Soup's chief engineer.
Applying these rules, a typical repairperson could follow the steps
needed to assure that the soup kettles were kept in good working order.

Another use of artificial intelligence is virtual reality. Just a few
years ago, virtual reality, a computer approach to demonstrating how
things worked, was considered a plaything. Today, it is being applied in

many places and used for many purposes, not least of which was for the movie *Jurassic Park* with its roaming dinosaurs. Boeing has used virtual reality for the design of aircraft. A virtual reality system that was built for Fujita, a Japanese construction firm, shows how to operate equipment where there is limited visibility and few expert operators. Another interesting application of virtual reality is the need doctors have for three-dimensional models, to be able to tell the difference between veins, bones, and muscles.

Virtual reality also has considerable potential as a tool for rapid, custom design of new products. This capability can affect industry, just as the computer reservation system did in the airline industry. Because the brain uses about half of its capability to perceive and understand information, the computer helps people feel at home when viewing virtual reality images. In Tokyo, Matsushita has developed a "virtual kitchen" as a selling tool because it allows a customer to move appliances around in the kitchen to get a feel for how they would look in his/her home.

To illustrate the potential of virtual reality, Eastman Kodak has used it to demonstrate how to run complicated injection molding machines. Imagine how this approach could be used at a board of directors meeting when discussing annual performance. We can only conjecture about the possible uses of computers in the future. It brings to mind the introduction of the typewriter that nobody thought would work.

Is Creative Problem-Solving Possible?

The idea of an individual gathering all pertinent facts, weighing them carefully, and then making the best decision may be far off. When a person is in a position to exercise discretion, "personal preferences" often determine the choice that is made. For example, there are two explanations of why Avis Inc. moved its international car rental headquarters from Boston to a Long Island suburb. In his book, *Up the Organization*,

Robert Townsend, the former Avis chairman, recalled that they wondered where a person from Mars would locate the headquarters of an international company in the car rental and leasing business. A key criterion would clearly be: near active domestic and international airports. So, Avis moved to Long Island, between JFK and La Guardia (airports), while the competition went to the tight island of Manhattan. Sometime later, Townsend's successor, Winston V. Morrow Jr., told the *Wall Street Journal* that wasn't quite how it happened. In fact, the switch came about because Townsend and another top official both lived on Long Island and had no desire to move to Manhattan.

Examples abound of how personal preference dictates a solution:

- A purchasing agent awards a contract to a supplier who wines and dines him on a lavish scale. He explains that he rejected lower bids to assure better quality and service.

- An executive hires an old school mate, in preference to a proven manager with much more experience, on the grounds that "she'll fit in better around here."

- A controller is concerned that a plan to decentralize the company would reduce his authority, so he hires a consultant to "prove" that the costs of such a move would outweigh the benefits.

International managers surveyed by the author—496 of them—were asked to rank 10 factors that are taken into account when solving problems. Rationality, or the use of formal logic, was ranked 8th of the 10 items. Perception, or the ability to correctly identify problems, was ranked at the top of the list by 82% of the managers, while compulsion, the need to get the job done at any cost, was considered the least desirable approach. This low regard for performance may be disturbing. However, this survey showed that senior managers typically prefer to use their ability to see and understand a problem rather than jumping to conclusions when looking for answers.

Professor Peer Solberg, an inspired researcher in decision-making, describes the final confirmation of a decision as an exercise in prejudice, of making sure that one's favorite solution indeed is chosen. Obviously, rational problem-solving alone does not account for what we observe in most situations. This is not to say that all problem-solving is purely subjective. In many situations, a subjective decision is not necessarily a bad one. If an individual has a high personal stake in a decision, it is more likely to be carried out successfully. The chairman's son-in-law might actually turn out to be the one with the managerial skills needed to save the company.

Personal preference can have a positive effect in problem-solving. For example, there is the case of a department head of a large conglomerate who was asked to lecture at a nearby university. However, company policy prohibited such non-business-related activities during working hours. The department head recalled that his manager had once expressed a desire to teach after his retirement. So, the department head prevailed on the university to invite them both to lecture. Not too surprisingly, when he requested permission to lecture at the university, his manager responded, When do we start?" Company rules were bent to accommodate personal preferences. Of course, personal preference leaves management on the horns of a dilemma. How can the powerful, motivating force of personal preference be utilized while avoiding the problems of power politics, influence-wielding, Machiavellian management, and personal convenience?

The power of creativity shows itself most distinctly in problem-solving. If we recognize that most areas of endeavor would benefit from greater use of creativity, then there would be greater emphasis on using it wherever possible. Individuals who know their Creative Intelligence styles would most likely apply them whenever possible. Creative problem solving would become an indispensable tool for finding answers to many problems.

The Brain: A Key to Understanding Creative Intelligence

Ideas about the human mind have varied throughout history. Plato thought the mind was inside the head, while Aristotle believed it was in the heart. René Descartes maintained that it was nonmaterial and separate from the brain tissue in the head. Descartes believed that consciousness was the evidence that we existed: "I think, therefore I am." Only in the last few years has science been able to actually see inside the living brain using Positron Emission Tomography (PET) scans to determine what happens in the brain during the thinking process. *Scientific American* devoted a whole issue to understanding how the developing field of Neuroscience will contribute to enhancing the ways in which we use our brains. From the early understanding of the brain to the current knowledge we now have, the future is incredible. Not only will we be able to repair the brain, but also work is being done on how to improve our use of memory, thinking, and the many functions that are so crucial to our well-being and to enhancing our creativity.

Creative Intelligence utilizes working memory as a basis for action and for putting thoughts and ideas together effectively. Creative Intelligence involves, in part, searches based on past experience. Dr. Salk's development of a polio vaccine relied on his previous experience with other vaccines.

Creative Intelligence involves brain functions that are required to perceive, understand, and be conscious of the world around us. Those who have studied the brain have long avoided the issue of consciousness and its relationship to the neural processes. Many believed that consciousness was too subjective to be "objective." Psychologists, on the other hand, based their conclusions on observing behavior to understand mental processes. The brain can relate current experience to past memories that are stored. An understanding of consciousness is important because it relates to "awareness." This is the process by which information is made available for use by the brain and is needed for Creative Intelligence.

The way in which the brain functions helps us to understand why there are different styles of Creative Intelligence. The four modes in which the brain operates also can be related to Creative Intelligence:

- Alpha—This mode of the brain's operation involves deep concentration and helps add to creative thought or insight. Often, this is the mode of the Imaginative style.

- Beta—This mode is typically used during conversation. Because of the rapid processing of information, there is less chance of creative thoughts being developed. In other words, "Keep your mouth shut if you want to be creative!" This mode is typical of the Intuitive Creative Intelligence style.

- Theta—In the theta mode, the brain operates at its slowest speed and may be at its most creative. Apparently, this mode facilitates the interaction of many ideas that ultimately lead to creative output. Thomas Edison and Henry Ford were supposed to have achieved their best ideas while in this mode. The Innovative style fits this category.

- Delta—The brain continues to function in the delta mode while we sleep. This helps us to organize thoughts and understanding. Also, recollection is often blocked during waking hours. Have you gone to bed with an "impossible" problem only to wake the next morning with a way to solve it? While this mode is not typical of any one style, it would most likely be either the imaginative or inspirational style because they both carry their ideas with them all the time.

How the Brain Functions

Understanding the brain and how it functions can be quite complex and daunting.

Anthropologist Melvin Konner believes that many human characteristics, from risk-taking to aggression, are strongly influenced by heredity. He sees a biological underpinning to most behavior. Some behavior can be modified or changed, while other behavior can be merely controlled. Another consideration is that our brain develops most during the early years of life. This has important implications for education and creativity.

Recent discoveries have shown that information, emotions, and language are part of a dynamic process that changes the pathways in the brain and is revised as needed. The brain's structure develops as the brain continues to interact with the world. Another consideration is the way in which genes affect a person's temperament, personality, and ability to learn. The gene that controls the brain's absorption of dopamine influences an individual's willingness to explore, become excitable, or be quick-tempered. This could also affect an individual's Creative Intelligence. While genes are not the sole basis for how the brain functions, they do have a critical impact on our personality. How we think and what we value have a direct effect on Creative Intelligence.

Understanding the Brain

Inspiration, insight, ingenuity, and originality are all related to the brain. Why do some ideas come in a "flash," and how do inquisitiveness, beliefs, values, and instinct control decisions that we make? One of the important aspects of Creative Intelligence is how a reliance on belief affects us when we deal with new or uncertain situations. Belief is critical in the sense that it forms the foundation that underlies reasoning. It is an important part of how we reach conclusions and how we treat new evidence. Belief also determines whether a given course of action will be accepted and how it will affect our underlying values. For creativity to flourish, an individual has to have a strong belief in what he or she proposes to do.

The Brain and Reality

The brain is our interface with reality. Interpretation, recognition, understanding, judgment, thinking, and many other aspects of Creative Intelligence are ultimately determined in the brain. Because of the many functions it performs, the brain and its modes of operation can be extremely complex. Candace Pert, at the National Institute of Mental Health, believes that the front portion of the brain is most critical to creative thought. The front part of the brain is where ideas are created and feelings and perceptions are interpreted to form our conscious awareness. The top outer portion of the brain is considered the center of perception and intelligence. Thus, a person's memories are, in effect, many combinations of these connections.

Canadian scientists who studied Einstein's brain believed that they found the basis for his genius. The size of Einstein's brain may have been average, but the portion that related to mathematical ability and spatial reasoning was significantly larger than average. Another finding was that a critical portion of his brain was smaller than average. This suggests that his brain cells were closer together than normal in that part of the brain, which allowed them to work together more effectively and handle enormous amounts of information. This combination of unique characteristics may account, in part, for Einstein's leaps of insight, which depended on visual images. He was able to intuitively translate these images into mathematical formulas.

The brain and its functioning contribute to a better understanding of our behavior. Knowledge about the brain helps to explain why we have multiple styles of Creative Intelligence. If we are able to understand the reasons behind why we think and behave the way we do, we will be in a better position to find more effective ways of using our Creative Intelligence. Although we know a great deal about the structure and functioning of the brain, each individual has a different, specific anatomy. These variations account for the differences we observe in people's behavior, especially in their Creative Intelligence. The manner in which brain cells interact seems to be determined at birth, and the speed of electrical activity in the brain appears to be determined by our genes.

5

APPLYING CREATIVITY TO EDUCATION

One approach to learning does not fit all and imposes rigidity and loss of creativity.

We live and learn and eventually we may learn to live.

You forget what you are told but may remember what you have seen. What you discover on your own stays with you longest.

Creativity in Education

The root of learning is being curious and able to wonder. **If people aren't curious, they won't experiment to see how the world really works. Curiosity is innate, but it can be encouraged by education that supports openness and questioning.** A lesson that is exciting makes an impact on the learner. Is it any wonder that lecturing is being questioned as the best way to encourage knowledge retention?

"Don't teach them; let them learn!" suggests that we need a more creative approach to education, learning, and training. If we allow students and participants to be open, to question new material presented, and to assert bold, new ideas, we will be on track to a better educational system. This in turn is important in helping students release their creative energy. Advanced educational institutions have shifted the emphasis from passing exams to providing mind-stretching experiences. They now encourage inquiry, exploration, questioning, and trying new approaches.

Can we introduce creativity into education? Have you ever wondered why in any given class there are many different responses to the ideas presented by the teacher? People have speculated that differences observed were because of different levels of intelligence. Is this the answer, or is it the case that some students are bored while others are keenly interested? In some instances, students are simply "turned off" by mathematics, while others consider it a challenge. How can we account for these differences, and can a more creative approach to education accommodate the students' different abilities?

All levels of education are struggling with the daunting challenge of how to improve the learning process. Learning signifies retention, understanding, and the ability to apply knowledge. Simply spending increasing amounts of money is not the answer, nor is focusing primarily on new ways of presenting material. **It is critical that we pay closer attention to how students retain the knowledge they have learned.**

Considerable effort has been devoted to improving education. Notwithstanding, lecturing is still the preferred mode of presenting information. Lecturing—telling students or participants what we want them to hear—does not ensure that learning takes place. Additionally, most exams do not measure true learning. Rather, exams tend to show what has been memorized. They rarely deal with integration, retention, and the understanding of knowledge.

How Education Is Viewed

Dr. Ken Robinson, a noted educator, has been knighted for his contribution to education. He has made a number of recommendations, not least of which was answering the question of where students will utilize their knowledge. Today's employers generally look for self-confident employees who can think intuitively, communicate effectively, and are imaginative, innovative, flexible, and able to work in teams. However, educational systems are not designed to produce graduates with these skills. To address this issue, educators have raised standards, but have not significantly changed the current curriculum. The system of higher education evolved in a time when there were different needs and social realities, and when college degrees were a mark of educational achievement and distinction. Current educational expectations must focus on specific vocational relevance or a variety of transferable skills based on the ability to adapt to new and changing requirements. This is a challenge that educational institutions can only solve by "thinking outside the box" and applying the concepts of creativity and adaptability.

Robinson recommends that in a complex and technologically oriented society, we should strongly consider the growing need for college graduates who have advanced intellectual skills that include the arts, language, and writing. We also need to broaden their thinking and skills in computers, mathematics, and science. Although former President Clinton stated that his intention was to make it possible for every high-school graduate to attend college, two important factors were not taken into account. First, nearly 30% of college students need at least one remedial class to bring them up to college-level work. Second, there are currently more college graduates than jobs that require college-level skills. As a consequence, many college graduates take jobs that do not fit their expertise.

Educational crusader Alfie Kohn thinks that school reforms that focus on standardized curriculum and standardized testing actually hinder the learning process. A former teacher, Kohn disputes the notion put forth that children need to learn a particular set of facts to be culturally literate and successful. Kohn focuses instead on a more creative approach that emphasizes thinking and understanding. He also believes that standardized approaches do not level the playing field for disadvantaged children, and that these so-called "progressive" approaches produce highly uneven results.

The Tradition of the Active Mind

Henry David Thoreau graduated from Harvard College in 1837 at the age of 20, and shortly thereafter, he became a schoolteacher. He left teaching just a few years later, largely because he was disillusioned with the conventional classroom, believing it prevented more learning than it facilitated. He wrote that education makes a straight-cut ditch of a free, meandering brook. He was one of the early educators who envisioned the need for a new and better approach to education.

Thoreau was a "philosopher of learning," and wrote about the subject eloquently and at length. He was an innovative teacher, taking students on a wide range of field trips—from nature walks to visiting local businesses. He encouraged the students to interpret what they saw, to formulate hypotheses and then test them. He was a model of intellectual curiosity, and was open to being proven wrong. He demonstrated a rare respect for the past and for other cultures, such as Native Americans. He believed that children learned when they were ready to learn, and that experience was the best teacher.

Thoreau engaged in and championed lifelong learning. Considered a pioneer in adult education, he regularly lectured on the lyceum circuit and was active in the transcendentalist movement. In addition, he analyzed the learning process itself in his personal journals. He explored the relationship between the mind and the physical world, between activity and analysis. The very process of writing helped him sort out and formulate his ideas. Thoreau constantly did battle with unthinkable routine that was supported by institutional inertia and blind authoritarianism. In discussing Harvard College, he said that it had all the branches of available knowledge, but none of the roots or background of knowledge.

Thoreau articulated his vision of what education could and should be in letters, along with a harsh denunciation of traditional practices such as corporal punishment. He believed passionately that education was not simply transmitting existing culture, but should creatively reconstruct it. He felt that education should be pleasant for the teacher and the student. Thoreau (along with friend and mentor, Ralph Waldo Emerson) envisioned a system of education that immersed each student in the complete cycle of experiencing, formulating, and then bringing formulations back into experience to test, hone, and modify them. He also saw education as a never-ending process.

Socrates, whose philosophy was recorded in the writings of his student Plato, had a special view of what it means to be educated. He considered an educated person to be one who could handle day-by-day circumstances and have the judgment to deal appropriately with problems. Most important was the idea that honor and decency helped to determine the manner in which an educated person interacted with others. He believed that human behavior should be guided by wisdom and self-control in the areas of pleasure, misfortune, and success. His focus was on an individual's virtues rather than on knowledge or intelligence.

Nearly 2,500 years after his death, Socrates' approach to learning is gaining wider acceptance. He relied on asking questions to stimulate critical thinking in his students, and to help them arrive at logical conclusions. His approach, referred to as the dialectic or Socratic method, encouraged discussion. He did not present answers, but led by questioning that resulted in what we now refer to as "discovery." After reasoning through a problem, students arrive at answers based on thinking through the data. This approach leads to more in-depth understanding, and thus, increased retention of knowledge.

Socrates' approach to teaching required that the teacher ask leading questions, allowing students to respond based on their knowledge and experience. The responses were then analyzed as part of the ensuing discussion. Conclusions resulted from reasoning rather than by being told the answers. Students "discovered" answers based on their own reasoning process.

Problems Confronting Education

The U.S. is currently facing a critical shortage of qualified teachers, especially in rural communities. This teacher shortage is expected to reach 2.7 million in the next decade, according to a study by the National Center for Education Statistics (NCES). To assure that we have a sufficient number of qualified teachers, we need to provide continuing education for those who are already in the system. Teachers need to keep up with the rapid pace of technological advancement and new instruction methods.

In 1998, Massachusetts administered certification exams to its teachers and approximately 60% failed to pass. This highlights a widespread problem in the competency level of teachers. Without competent teachers, we cannot expect students to learn in a manner that fulfills their potential. We expect dedication, commitment, competence, and unflagging energy from teachers. Our ability to attract and retain such highly qualified educators depends, in part, on being able to adequately compensate them for their efforts. Teachers spend an extraordinary amount of time preparing for their classes. Considering that bright, young minds have myriad opportunities and choices in the work they might pursue, we need to make teaching intellectually rewarding and, at the same time, recognize the impact of currently inordinate shortfalls in compensation.

Another consideration in assuring highly qualified educators is to recognize their need for lifelong learning. For example, information technology professionals spend a significant amount of time just keeping up with new technological developments. To stay in the loop, they attend classes, use online learning, and read current books and other material. In addition, they network with colleagues and volunteer for projects that strengthen their skills.

In general, today's educational system is based on an unbalanced curriculum that emphasizes science, technology, mathematics, and language. The arts and humanities are de-emphasized. To assure a more creative environment, there needs to be a balance among all areas of education. An unbalanced curriculum ultimately leads to an unbalanced education. In turn, a rigid curriculum assumes that there are distinctive domains of knowledge required and that the ideas, knowledge, and skills that are taught can provide the education needed for our emerging society.

Problems in U.S. education are not limited to poor, inner-city schools. Affluent school districts are also failing to provide what students need to learn to be successful. Students are not being challenged, nor are they being asked to stretch their minds. American students increasingly lag behind students in several Asian and European countries in standardized tests. To overcome this deficiency, schools need to focus on effective written and oral communication skills and embrace a creative approach to learning. Students need a solid foundation in literature and the social sciences, with special emphases on history and geography. In addition, while the classic Euro-centric approach to what is covered in the classroom has value, it should also include the rest of the world.

Long ago, Africa recognized the importance of home and community. The people who live there recognized that it requires a whole village to contribute to raising a child. In modern society, this is an enormous challenge, as families and communities face unprecedented disruptions. However, without communities playing a significant role in supporting education, we will not have a stable society. It is unrealistic to expect our educational institutions to accomplish this goal alone.

How Do We Learn?

We learn best by doing, in contrast to sitting and listening. Practice helps us to understand and effectively retain knowledge. To a great extent, knowledge retention depends on reinforcement that uses multiple examples. Being exposed to new material only once generally is not sufficient to assure long-term retention. A number of approaches have been used to assure knowledge retention. Research by Dr. Martin Taft, a long-time educator, introduced a more creative approach that uses information reinforcement to increase retention. He found that when specific chunks of knowledge are repeated throughout a course, rote memorization of material becomes unnecessary. Reinforcement literally helps to "internalize" knowledge and makes it a part of the individual's thought process. Also, when a student is directly involved with actual problems, this helps him or her retain new knowledge.

Gary Locke, governor of the state of Washington, discussed the need for lifelong learning in his address to the top high school graduates of 1998. He feels that we live in the Information Age, and that what will drive our economy is knowledge, creativity, and imagination. Education is supported by taxpayers and individuals paying tuition. Thus, both the public at large and individual citizens have high stakes in assuring the best possible education.

A significant problem confronting our educational system is the orientation toward preparing students for a single career. In reality, most people have multiple careers during their working lives. This suggests the need for lifelong learning. Because a change in occupation generally requires new knowledge, we should look for innovative ways to make it available. Computers and distance learning can contribute to meeting continuing education needs.

The quality of learning will increasingly take precedence over the name of the school one attends. The key to success will be the ability to build on previous knowledge and to generate new and creative ideas. At the outset, we need to recognize that everyone is different because of genetic makeup, background influences, preferences, Creative Intelligence, and perhaps most important, personality. **How is it possible for teachers—no matter how conscientious or skilled—to address the differences with which they are confronted?** Yet this is precisely the situation facing educators every day in the classroom. Another consideration is the influence of well-meaning parents who inadvertently keep a child from pursuing the career he or she really wants. Consider, for example, the physician who wanted to be a musician and formed a quartet after becoming a doctor, or the young accountant who desperately wanted to be an artist but whose mother told her that artists don't make any money. How often do well-meaning parents cope with a precocious child who appears unruly but who really only wants to pursue his or her own agenda? **At what point is creativity stifled, and how do we distinguish the unruly child from the one who is simply bored.** Examples abound of famous people who were largely self-taught, including Abraham Lincoln, and others who were totally bored in school, such as Newton and Einstein.

How Education Is Changing

To be effective, education must change to meet the radically new environment in which it operates. If you examine the "intellectual assumptions" on which our system of education was built, it becomes obvious that to improve education, consideration has to be given to a number of factors: first are the educators; second is the curriculum and which courses should be required; and third are the physical facilities, which must be conducive to learning. Fortunately, the emphasis in education is moving toward greater involvement by the students. The change encourages questioning and setting up conditions for discovery and inventiveness.

The ability to use knowledge is another critical aspect of learning. One example is a German equipment manufacturer that has its new machinists spending six months filing a piece of steel until it is absolutely square. During this process, the machinists develop the ability to recognize true quality in the work they will be doing. They learn!

Educator Leslie Hart's concern with how to improve education led her to recognize the need to understand learning. She suggests that teachers can be much more effective if they understand key aspects of how we think. As a start, teachers can build on our natural pattern-seeking ability. Hart describes the way in which small children make sense of the world by putting things and people into categories, and suggests that teachers exploit this strong, innate tendency. Children in the 5th and 6th grades responded to her questions by being quite innovative. For example, they were asked how to keep milk from turning sour. Their response was to leave it in the cow. Or, when asked what is the cause of dust, they responded by saying that janitors were the main cause. Another question they were asked was what does a census-taker do? They said he or she increases the population as he/she goes from house to house.

Hart suggests that we need to determine how knowledge is retained. Her suggestion was that we use goal-oriented sequences to enhance teaching effectiveness. She maintains that after learning how to perform a task, we become better with practice, and that knowledge stored is later automatically used. She makes a number of recommendations for teaching that rely on understanding how the brain functions. Her approach recognizes that support and encouragement facilitate learning, while fear shuts it down. Young children need to verbalize while they learn to touch and learn in their own way and they learn more quickly if lessons are tied to their reality. Hart suggests that intuition, creativity, and pattern-seeking processes need to be encouraged as ways to improve learning.

Recognizing that we are all different, Dr. Mel Levine, founder of the All Kinds of Minds Foundation, believes we need to teach the way individual children learn. Levine's approach is to tailor teaching techniques to learning ability. For example, a child who learns best by using words might be encouraged to increase his or her reading comprehension. This is accomplished by having the student write a summary after each assignment. That child might have trouble with math unless the teacher focuses on verbal explanations. Another child with weaker verbal skills and who learns from images, might need help with reading. By giving students sets of questions to answer about a text, this would align their learning style with the material being covered. Levine also suggests that to assure comprehension of mathematics, each child should try to solve math problems by themselves in order to learn the basic concepts.

New Approaches to Learning

Many states have plans to enhance math and science education, with greater emphasis on critical-reasoning skills. According to Gerald F. Wheeler of the National Science Teachers Association, when we drill students and use lectures covering a long list of facts, this just doesn't produce thinking adults. Where hands-on learning is used, it leads to a better understanding of the fundamental principles of math and science. A number of U.S. schools are adopting a hands-on approach to teaching science. For instance, in one school, third graders were asked to construct simple switching circuits with batteries and bulbs to learn about electricity; fourth graders built musical instruments out of metal bars and strings. Another school had a science center with robots, a wind tunnel, a full-scale laboratory, and a planetarium—all funded by the Bayer Corporation.

Another issue affecting U.S. math and science performance is the fact that currently; about 25% of teachers have not majored in the subjects they are teaching. A group of school districts near Chicago has taken a new approach to teaching mathematics with impressive results. Instead of traditional class lectures and testing, students work in teams to solve problems and learn from their mistakes. These students scored among the top five countries around the world, whereas the U.S. as a whole ranked considerably lower. The name for this form of teaching is *discovery learning*. It involves hands-on education, or inquiry-based teaching, which contributes to increased creativity. The most dramatic gain is for the average student, who is often left behind when taught by traditional methods.

Psychology professor Joann Farver at the University of Southern California has undertaken an innovative approach to helping her students connect coursework to the real world. In her psychology class, students are required to work in the field several hours a week, putting theory into practice. Students take turns lecturing and facilitating discussions in class, and report that they are challenged and stimulated by the experience.

An important consideration in education is how can we assure understanding of ideas and concepts in contrast to memorizing factual material? Understanding depends on the way in which material is presented and explained. Graphic illustrations, slides, and films can facilitate understanding and retention. The ultimate goal of a good education should be to use the knowledge learned and to encourage creative approaches that would utilize one's Creative Intelligence.

Introducing Change in Education

In the spring of 1992, the University of California at Los Angeles Academic Senate Subcommittee on Undergraduate Education held a retreat to focus on how to enhance the undergraduate experience. Faculty members, administrators, and student representatives attended the retreat. A number of ideas and recommendations were generated. There were three basic goals: increasing teacher/student interaction, developing innovative approaches to teaching and curriculum (including students in the development process), and creating a campus culture in which undergraduates could thrive. The Senior Vice Chancellor for Academic Affairs, Richard Sisson, summarized the results of the retreat by his statement that it is important for all students to have the experience of creating something while they're at the university. His expectation was that every major would experience discovery in the classroom that was a creative expression appropriate to the major. Discovery, in this sense, is not only an adventure into how knowledge is formed, but assists in the identity of one's self.

The University of Southern California is experimenting with a new approach to teaching math. As a starting point, it was implemented in a class called Calculus for Business. In the past, students had three hours of lecture and one hour of discussion each week. The lectures consisted primarily of professors working out problems on the board and then sending the students off with homework assignments. The new method cuts lecture time in half. It devotes the remaining class time to working on and discussing math problems with the students. There is also an online component that provides an instant tutorial if students make errors. Feedback from the students has been very positive.

Jaime Escalante introduced an innovative approach to teaching math. The noted educator had remarkable success in East Los Angeles. He believed that disadvantaged students were capable of learning math and he worked hard to see that they did. He used innovative teaching methods, including visual aids, mind games, and peer pressure. He met with students before and after school, and got their parents involved when students didn't do their part, as he saw it. In one case, the parent of a truant student failed to return repeated calls. Undeterred, he called at 5 a.m. to be sure to catch the student's father at home. The result was that the student came back to school!

Japanese educator Tori Kumon believes that all children are born with enormous potential to learn. His method of teaching math utilizes sequenced worksheets. A child moves on to the next worksheet only after demonstrating proficiency on the prior one, and must meet a standard completion time for each worksheet. The sequence of 3,800 worksheets covers everything from basic arithmetic through integral calculus. Repetition is a key aspect of the system's design. This approach steadily builds each student's confidence and has led to very effective results.

Differences in Students

An important aspect of teaching is recognizing that each individual has different levels of cognitive complexity (the ability to recognize and understand various cues) and different levels of Creative Intelligence. There are individuals who easily recognize cues and complex figures, while others struggle in the same situations. Some individuals are good at the use of symbols and can manipulate mathematical formulas with ease. Others struggle with symbols and are never fully comfortable with them. Some individuals prefer graphic or pictorial representations, whereas others prefer specific facts. Some individuals reach conclusions easily based on a set of facts, while others totally miss the point.

How can a teacher deal with all these differences in a single classroom? One attempt was to have "honors" or "advanced" classes open to those with good grades in prior courses. This approach recognized that differences exist. Where possible, groups could be chosen that had comparable cognitive complexity to be included in special classes. The teacher could then focus on using material that matched a student's preferred learning style. This also implied that the subject matter would be tailored to the way in which students could best understand and retain the knowledge.

In addition to the tailoring of teaching methods to match learning styles, education needs to encourage more openness and creativity. For example, in one class, a teacher gives extra credit for answers on exams that include the "right" answers *plus* "alternative" answers proposed by the student. In a chemistry class at the University of Southern California, the professor does not give students formulas for chemical reactions, but rather uses a "discovery" approach that forces students to try to find the answers. Afterward, the professor shows the reason why the correct answer works, and why others do not. This approach helps the students understand and remember the chemical formulas.

Experiential learning centers have been used to study the behavior of students under different learning conditions. The centers consist of one-way glass with video cameras to record what's happening. They also have voice communication with the students. In one experiment, a class was separated into four learning categories based on personality types. The relationship of individual learning styles to how each student approached problem-solving soon became obvious. The intuitive students solved a problem given to the class in 15 minutes, even though they were allowed one hour to complete the exercise. The innovative students took the full hour and proposed a number of alternatives. The imaginative group never completed the exercise, even though they were given several warnings on time remaining. The inspirational group focused on the human impact of alternate solutions. Rather than proposing direct answers, they set conditions for the solution based on human or societal impact. This experiment clearly showed the differences in learning styles based on different Creativity Intelligence styles. When a video of the exercise was played back for the entire class, they laughed when they saw how each style demonstrated certain characteristics and how they compared with each other.

Learning Theory

Learning theory considers the "amount" learned over a given time period, but does not specifically consider the level of comprehension, as shown in Figure 5–1. **Testing is used as the basis to determine whether a subject matter has been adequately covered. In general, this approach does not determine how much knowledge has been retained, or for how long**. The moment that a test is over, forgetting begins. How often do students leaving a test say, "Thank goodness I'll never have to see that subject again!" This can hardly be construed as learning.

Subjects such as calculus can be taught in a way such that "basic concepts" are retained even though complex formulas are not. Generally, only professionals such as engineers, mathematicians, and scien-

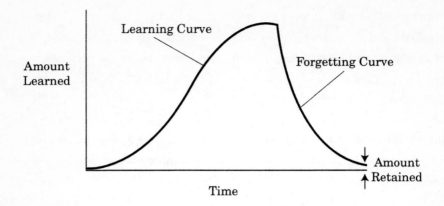

Learning/Forgetting

FIGURE 5-1   Level of comprehension.

tists need a working knowledge of formulas to solve everyday problems. Students are sometimes lost when trying to follow a lecture that could use a graphic approach to better explain underlying theory. The current view of learning theory is that students gain more from actual experience and interaction with their fellow students than from passively sitting and listening to lectures. This "constructivist" theory is useful when designing technology-based learning systems. The developers of the theory, Clark Chinn and William Brewer, suggest that there is a need for a learning model based on conceptual change. This approach sequences instruction in a way that helps students abandon their previous beliefs and accept new ideas. While Chinn and Brewer have focused on science instruction, other subject areas can benefit from this approach as well. Students have to justify their reasoning and become actively involved in the issues at hand.

To encourage "deep processing" of ideas, a sequential model for instruction is recommended. The first step is to have the students state their beliefs and assumptions prior to being faced with new information. As new information is introduced, students are then asked to discuss and evaluate the information and work on constructing new theories for themselves. Students attempt to predict the outcome of an experiment, construct a competing theoretical explanation that supports their prediction, observe the actual outcome, and evaluate and modify their original predictions and the competing explanations.

Dr. Richard Mann, who has studied the learning process, suggests that the Chinn and Brewer model would be ideal for social science instruction. He suggests that a student would start with a case study or other experiential activity. That would be followed by readings and presentations of new information. The student would then examine the material and use it as the basis for participating in a group discussion. Additional case studies would then be introduced that demonstrate the application of the new material learned and show how it could be used.

For students to understand economics, Kathryn Robinson of Chaffin Junior High School in Arkansas applies the basic principles by showing how they affect decisions the students will be making. She relies on examples from the current literature to demonstrate that there are always tradeoffs involved in making choices. She then relates how these examples apply to the students' everyday lives.

Situated learning also relates past knowledge to what is covered in the classroom. As shown by Jean Lave, this approach to understanding relates applications to ones in a real-life context. Lave has found that student-directed learning environments provide the ideal climate for learning. For this approach to work, students are arranged in small groups and make decisions about actual problems. Projects are then used that test their decisions. Learning takes place based on the actions that result from the students' decisions. **Learning is further enhanced when there is interaction and collaboration among students.**

Testing and Learning

For students interested in lifelong learning, Wayne Jennings points out that there is little correlation between test scores and the fundamental goal of developing responsible citizens. Walt Gardner, a long time teacher, who has written numerous op-ed articles, asserts that testing isn't the problem. Rather, it is the limitations of standardized tests that are at fault. He recommends that to be meaningful, tests need to measure what children have learned in class, rather than what they already knew when they came to school. From another perspective, Larry Hoffner maintains that standardized tests fail to recognize the diversity of student learning and academic growth. He recommends that testing should be flexible and take into account the backgrounds of students. From another perspective, standardized tests are only useful in measuring basic competencies, not in measuring higher levels of learning that require more in-depth performance assessment.

The Relationship Between Math and Music

Interestingly, there are important connections between math and music. Each field has produced child prodigies, and there are numerous instances of individuals with talent in both fields. Einstein played the violin; Saint-Saëns enjoyed mathematics. Physicist Gordon Shaw cites evidence that the brain can be primed to handle mathematical problems by listening to Mozart.

There have been questions about the benefit of increasing the amount of math homework that students are required to do. Increasing homework showed an improvement in Japan, but a drop in scores in Canada, Germany, and the U.S. This leads one to the conclusion that a brute-force approach, which piles homework on students, doesn't work. **If we improve teaching methods, it may actually be possible to reduce the amount of work a student has to do outside of school.**

A working knowledge of mathematics is considered important for almost everyone in daily life. Generally, this would include an understanding of the basics of statistics and algebra. In addition, an understanding of the physical sciences, with special emphasis on environmental issues, will increasingly be needed in the future to understand our daily lives. Even rudimentary scientific knowledge can be useful in knowing how to handle household waste to understanding the implications of issues such as global warming. Also, we cannot overlook the importance of art and music appreciation. The arts enrich the lives of all of us and are important to stimulating creativity. A good understanding of government and the economy is essential for developing an informed citizenry, as is a broad understanding of the issues supporting physical health and wellness.

Most importantly, in this complex world of ours, schools need to teach creative problem-solving skills. Critical thinking and the ability to focus on important issues need to be top priorities.

The Environment and Education

In order to increase creative potential in education, we need to emphasize "mind-expanding" experiences. In the rapidly changing environment we are now experiencing, students need open minds to deal with the many difficult problems they encounter. Given these considerations, we need to encourage inquisitiveness and a willingness to develop new approaches to problems. Mind-expanding experiences require an educational environment in which inquiry, exploration, and questioning replace an emphasis on facts or knowledge that may no longer be applicable.

An "open" learning environment, in many cases, is a radical departure from current educational approaches. To improve education, teaching will have to change so that the emphasis is on understanding and learning. That is not to say that there is anything wrong with knowing factual material. It is a matter of emphasis. Understanding the meaning of what has been learned and knowing where and how to use that knowledge would lead to a better-educated society and a more "creative" populace.

Can Computers Enhance Education?

In the current computer era, knowledge, information, and learning have become increasingly interdependent. Without the Internet, most of us would be at a loss to find needed information. The use of computers can provide an opportunity to rethink education and move beyond lecture-based teaching.

The unique powers of the computer can support a learning experience that includes a number of innovative approaches. Computers provide easy access to information using the Internet and have the potential of facilitating how information is presented. Computers can also support the educational process with multimedia presentations. Peter Drucker, a noted educator, has suggested that use of the Internet for continuing adult education could become one of our greatest growth industries. Considering that the amount of money spent on education is on the order of $1 trillion per year, there is room for more creative approaches than are currently being used. New growth will most likely be at the college level and in adult education, as well as the need for specialized training courses for industry and the government. The Elderhostel program is an example of the exponential growth of courses for retired people who want to continue their education.

A creative approach to learning would deal with the high cost of tuition that is making education more difficult to obtain for many students. An increasing number of schools are turning away qualified students because they cannot accommodate them. Another factor that needs to be considered is that more students are working and can only attend school part-time. They would benefit from computer-based distance learning and in many cases, distance learning has been shown to improve the student's learning experience. The improvement is due, in part, to the student's ability to easily review course material when concepts are not understood.

Distance learning is most effective when students are given career testing prior to entering a program. This allows them to focus on coursework that best suits their cognitive ability. Material can be presented to students at various locations, and faculty can use interactive lectures, followed by exercises that reinforce learning the material presented. Case studies can help students understand the application of the material learned to real-life problems. Where it is deemed important, students can meet with the professor to have eye contact on a regular basis, such as once a week or at another appropriate interval. To assist the student, chat rooms on the Internet can facilitate interaction with the professor and among students. Students can also be required to make presentations to demonstrate that they know how to use the knowledge gained.

Online education is gaining in popularity because of its flexibility and efficient use of time. However, concern has been expressed regarding quality control, the value of school affiliations, validity and acceptance of degrees, and the changing dynamics of learning. Ideally, small online classes allow extensive interaction between teachers and students, but there are also the dangers of isolation and the loss of spontaneity, collaboration and sharing of ideas. Proponents of the virtual learning experience believe that lectures are a thing of the past. **Flexibility is an important reason for the growth of online learning.** It meets the needs of people living in isolated communities and students who simply enjoy the freedom to choose courses when they want them rather than being limited to specific hours at a university. A major benefit of online education is improving the ratio of students to teachers. This could readily replace the mega-section classes that often have several hundred students in attendance at one time.

It is important to recognize that distance learning works for some students but not for all. Jill-Marie Bauer of Baker College in Flint, Michigan teaches writing both online and in a classroom. She reports that students in a classroom who attend class but rarely participate can still get by, but students who don't participate in online discussions lose so much that they generally drop out. She also reports that her online students have tended to do somewhat better on tests that were given to both groups, but acknowledges that may be due to the fact that online students are generally older, more motivated, and more disciplined. Some students report that they do not like online courses because there is much less interaction with other students and less opportunity to learn from others. An example of the acceptance of distance learning is the Stanford Center for Professional Development (SCPD), which offers over 250 online continuing education courses in computer science and engineering. Over 6,000 professionals per year take advantage of this program to update their technical knowledge or work toward advanced degrees without interrupting the momentum of their careers. Students log onto courses via Internet browsers. Course material is either broadcast live or made available immediately following class. Students can choose from a list of course contents and have the opportunity of viewing videos along with graphics, as well as course notes and other materials. Tutoring with live interaction is available, allowing access to both professors and teaching assistants.

The Role of Technology in Education

Professor, Sir Douglas Hague of Oxford University believes that the role of higher education must be reconsidered in light of the advent of the "knowledge industries." Recognizing that the best and brightest minds are often in business rather than academia, he suggests that higher education needs to shift from traditional lectures to a variety of technology-aided teaching methods. Teachers need to become educational consultants, helping students discover knowledge on their own. Borrowing from the work of Cambridge University anthropologist Ernest Geller, Hague suggests that students need special job-related training following standardized education at the high school level. Hague envisions a more modular approach to education, spread out over people's careers.

Access to high-quality, low-cost education is more important now than ever before. Higher education needs to follow the lead of the business community and automate if it is to remain effective. Smith and Debenham developed an interactive computer software program that can automate the teaching process, and at the same time act as a personal tutor. The design criteria of the software was based on cognitive learning theory. Supplemental material that emphasizes key terms and concepts is used to enhance textbook assignments. This approach to teaching is individualized to fit a student's learning style and pace. Students are allowed to retake tests until they have achieved mastery of the material, and the system maintains comprehensive records of their progress.

There are several advantages to this type of computer-assisted instruction, including monitoring, pacing, and the elimination of cramming for tests. Students receive immediate feedback during tests, providing explanations of their errors. This approach has demonstrated that retention can be enhanced. The retest feature reduces anxiety and allows teachers to spend more time with students and less time correcting exams.

Students reported significant improvements in learning and retention when this type of computer-assisted learning supplemented traditional classroom instruction. Most students found the software easy to use, although access to the computer was a problem at times. Some of the students felt the software took too much of their study time, while others found it to be effective for understanding and learning. Students generally wanted to continue using the system and agreed that it helped them grasp terms and concepts more thoroughly than solely by reading textbooks. Students who demonstrated that they had computer mastery went on to tutor other students who were having problems. One requirement was that students had to put their knowledge to work on real-world problems and engage in internships.

Teacher Involvement with Distance Learning

Building on curiosity, self-learning, experimentation, exploration, and above all, questioning is the hallmark of truly advanced education. It is also the foundation for assuring enhanced creativity. An example of advances taking place in the use of distance learning is a high school English teacher who facilitated online discussions about reading assignments. These discussions, in turn, helped students develop topics for writing assignments. Students were able to clarify what was expected in their class assignments from Web sites instead of having to speak directly with the teacher.

The electronic classroom supports student-centered learning. Students can take ownership of the learning process once the teacher has provided the course description, syllabus, and assessment tools online. Using electronic media, teachers have an opportunity to enhance communication with both parents and students. **Because of their versatility, classroom Web sites can broaden a student's use of the Internet to include educational material along with games or chat rooms.**

At the University of Southern California, chemistry is now being taught with the aid of the Internet. Software is available that shows molecules, along with other particles, in three-dimensional representations, and allows the rotation and manipulation of these images to demonstrate their complex structures and shapes. Although many schools have invested considerable funds for computers and Internet connections, most teachers do not take full advantage of the available technology. In subjects such as chemistry, demonstrating what happens to molecules during chemical reactions is very difficult on a blackboard, but relatively simple using interactive Web pages.

Technology by itself does not automatically improve education. Rather, new approaches to education are needed if we are to utilize the Internet as part of the learning process. Traditionally, teachers took responsibility for delivering knowledge to students, who were then supposed to comprehend and retain it. However, today's students have ready access to libraries and information online. This change means that teachers have a new role that is more like that of a coach or guide. Using the Internet, teachers will have more time to work with students on research and evaluation skills. In addition, the Internet can help students understand how best to use the information they find. This approach encourages students to become more active in directing their own learning. The term "learner" or "participant" is often used to describe a student who is actively involved in such a process.

The U.S. Department of Education continues to conduct research regarding ways in which technology can enhance education. It considers a technology's effectiveness in supporting student achievement to be a key factor. Individual states that request federal funds for technology are required to submit long-range strategic plans dealing with 15 factors, including: how to improve student learning, what the requirements are for developing distance learning, how the teacher's and administrator's technological literacy will be enhanced, how the proposed system addresses the needs of low-income schools and students, and finally, how the involvement of parents will be increased. Obviously, these are important steps for incorporating technology into teaching, but we need to include inquisitiveness, openness, and challenging ideas that are presented and the use of creative thinking as integral parts of a curriculum. Half of the federal funds for technology are scheduled to go to states that are subject to the Title I formula for basic program money. The other half will be allocated based on how well the proposals show a long-term strategic plan that is likely to lead to educational improvement.

Alternative Schools

The Accelerated School (TAS) is a model that was developed by Stanford University's Dr. Henry Levin, and is a leading example of school reform and improved academic achievement. The key to this model is the underlying assumption that every student has potential. Consequently, standards are set very high. Teachers work to challenge each student with relevant and meaningful learning experiences; time-killing exercises have no place in this system. **Giving students problem-solving tools and knowledge prepares them to solve new problems with ever-increasing independence and open-minded, creative thinking.**

The three core principles used at TAS are: unity of purpose, empowerment coupled with responsibility, and building on strengths. The curriculum includes language arts, mathematics, science, social studies, visual and performing arts, physical education, and technology. Students are all on the same accelerated track, regardless of ability, but those who need it are given individual support. Both national and state curriculum standards are taken into consideration, and active involvement is expected from students, parents, teachers, staff, administrators, and members of the community. All lessons have themes that help students relate what they are learning in school to their interaction with the outside world. Cultural diversity is reflected in reading lists and exercises. Real-life experiences are included to reinforce skills and knowledge. In addition to technology, the arts are considered an integral part of the learning environment.

One of the measures of success for TAS was the performance on the Stanford 9 Assessments as compared with scores from the Los Angeles Unified School District (LAUSD). For fourth graders, every score at TAS was higher than any of the neighboring schools. Scores were significantly higher in both math and reading.

In 1995, Milwaukee, Wisconsin School Superintendent Howard Fuller and others worked aggressively to make fundamental changes that they hoped would improve the quality of education in the 15th largest school district in the country. Milwaukee was one of the earliest districts to try school vouchers, which give public funds to private schools and give parents a choice as to which schools their children will attend. Educational reforms of the 1970s and 1980s had mixed results, but generally point to the fact that money alone isn't the key to quality education. Reform needs to come from within communities, and for that to happen, the power of central administrations must be lessened significantly.

Where Do We Go from Here?

The introduction of creativity in education is sorely needed. Industry, government agencies, or any group that needs constant updating in its field and needs to stay abreast of the latest ideas in management, technology, or social responsibility also needs access to more creative approaches. Many of the ideas described for improving education in the classroom are applicable to any endeavor where change is endemic.

Another important area of study that has not had sufficient attention is the subject of ethics. We have seen this in the problems confronting Wall Street and executives who have tampered with their books to show higher earnings. The question is can we teach ethics or is this the responsibility of the home? Perhaps, a story that is told about Winston Churchill can illustrate the way in which education can contribute to a better understanding of ethical behavior. Churchill as a child was caught in a mud pond. A nearby farmer saved him from a certain death. Churchill's father offered to reward the farmer for saving his son. The farmer turned it down saying that he had to do it. Churchill's father then said that he would give the farmer's son the same education that his son would enjoy. As fate would have it, the farmer's son turned out to be Dr. Fleming who invented penicillin. This medication saved Winston Churchill who had pneumonia and would probably have died without the drug. Ethics had a way of paying off!

The major difference between education in schools and industry or government is in the emphasis on basic knowledge and thinking skills. In industry, the emphasis is on upgrading current skills or knowledge to have more effective workers. **Today there is an additional require-**

ment: to make organizations more open and creative. For this, the Creative Potential Profile is an invaluable tool for identifying those in the organization that are best suited for given occupations. This is especially true where workers have been out of school for a long period of time. For example, real-estate agents could not function today without the support of computers. Accountants would be at a loss without computers. Banks could not function without the use of computers. Manufacturing and distribution increasingly rely on customer relations and following sales trends and supplier contact.

Increasing morale and making performance more effective require continuing education for almost every segment of our society. To maintain our competitive position in the world, innovation and creativity are crucial. Organizations that ignore this requirement will soon be relics of the past. Survival and growth depend on greater use of learning; not training that simply copies what others are doing.

Creativity is indeed the panacea that can help us survive as a vital nation and remain competitive in a world where low-cost labor has driven us out of many fields. We need to face the challenge and take the bull by the horns.

6

THE CHALLENGE OF THE FUTURE

For those who live in the past, there is no future.

"If you take no part in the design of your future, it will be designed for you by others."

—*Edward de Bono*

Drivers of the Future

The environment in which we live is changing rapidly and in unpredictable ways. Individuals who are creative are able to bring about change and visualize future opportunities. **Creative leaders are a critical resource needed to find answers to difficult problems.** They are the ones who can navigate the future. They are able to embrace ambiguity and reframe problems as opportunities. They have competencies that include how to read and understand the environment, build alliances, recognize the importance of social responsibility, manage complexity, use information technology, and encourage creativity. Increasingly, leaders are using a proactive stance in taking their organizations into uncharted territory.

Leaders are willing to confront adversity, but in no situation should they be the end of the line. They must continuously interact with their

117

constituencies, whether in politics, production, education, religion, and so on. Each of these groups has its own opinion about what is desirable. They influence what a leader can do. Like a tightrope acrobat, the leader balances on a slender wire, where any misstep can result in disaster. **Effective leaders are willing to take risks, think outside the box, and recognize that empowerment provides a sense of ownership to stakeholders that helps to assure proposed changes will be accepted**.

An insightful view of leadership is found in *The Contrarian's Guide to Leadership,* a book co-authored by Dr. Stephen Sample, President of the University of Southern California, and Distinguished Professor Warren Bennis. They discuss the need to open vistas not previously explored or accepted. Contrarian leaders do not follow the pack. They believe in their own ideas of what is best. However, they listen openly and are responsive to new ideas, and are willing to constantly adjust their position in response to impending change. They also know the value of creative contributions from employees. A single innovation was what led to Intel's microprocessor. This is the kind of quantum jump that can be achieved by motivated employees.

Warren Bennis, a leader in the field of leadership, has published numerous books and articles on the subject. He conducted a research study with Robert Thomas in which they found that extraordinary leaders are the ones who have the skills needed to conquer adversity and emerge stronger because of it. Their research also showed that great leaders have the ability to create a sense of inclusion, where people share meaning with one another. These leaders have a distinct ability to communicate with a compelling voice that inspires a strong sense of values. Strong leaders are able to transcend adversity and reinvent themselves. They learn from their ordeals and have the perseverance to carry on even under adversity. Other factors that describe great leaders include knowing how to interact with people to gain commitment and having the ability to recognize what is important to members of an organization that make them feel a sense of excitement where all want to join in.

Leaders understand that creative ideas require recognition for those who are willing to stick their necks out. The difference between creative and non-creative people often depends on their willingness to take risks. Inventors such as Thomas Edison immersed themselves in their work and carried out hundreds of unsuccessful experiments before finding ones that worked. Individuals considered geniuses also turned out to be very hard workers, often producing a high volume of work. What these geniuses had in common was a deep understanding of their area of expertise, along with an ability to recognize anomalies that most people miss. They also were highly motivated and able to concentrate on problems or ideas for long periods of time.

Leaders who focus on encouraging and supporting their organizations to achieve new products and ideas will be the ones who will be out in front. Richard Lewis, founder and past CEO of Accountants Overload, balanced his inspirational style with his imaginative style. He was described by his employees as warmly enthusiastic, imaginative, and as having a flair for problem-solving. He constantly looked for ways to encourage and reward people. Lewis decided to make every employee a manager. With his senior management team, he developed what he termed "Chairman's Projects." He placed employees in leadership roles as project managers even though they had no prior experience in those positions. With his many ideas and a genuine desire to encourage his employees to be creative, he produced an environment in which innovation was a day-to-day activity. Organizations that have a strong interest in promoting creativity are the ones that become more competitive.

Successful leaders take moribund companies and turn them around so that they become viable, productive entities. Examples include Lou Gerstner at IBM, Lee Iacocca at Chrysler, and Jack Welch at GE. All exuded confidence, enthusiasm, and energy, and relied on a vision that could bring about desired change. Charisma is obviously a desirable trait in a leader, but by itself, it is not sufficient to assure desired outcomes. Studies have shown that, at best, all a leader can achieve is perhaps a 25–30% improvement after taking into account the impact of industry and economic factors. The question then is how does a strong, charismatic leader recognize the importance of bringing the organization along with his or her vision. Jack Welch at GE was willing to "lay waste" to parts of the company so that the remaining units would have a greater chance of success. This assured that the least profitable units would not encumber the units that would move GE ahead.

Responding to fierce global competition, Jack Welch focused GE's efforts in areas where he felt the company could be number one or two in the world, and gave up on all other divisions of the company. He introduced an employee "Workout Program" that used a form of town meeting, where employees could share ideas and make suggestions. In turn, managers were required to make decisions on the spot. In this kind of open environment, GE was able to correct many of its problems in a timely fashion.

Other companies have also set up informal work systems and networks for generating and sharing ideas. This approach fosters teamwork, which can contribute to huge dividends. Team members not only learn from each other, but also are able to generate better ideas together than they could separately. An important benefit of the team approach is that when a member leaves, his or her knowledge does not leave as well. An additional benefit of investing in team members is to help them increase their knowledge so they are encouraged to stay with the company.

How Creative Leaders Function

A leader's creative style and Creative Intelligence will often determine the likelihood of successful change. The intuitive-style leader often introduces change by announcing it. The response to this approach generally creates rigidity. The inspirational leader, on the other hand, discusses change, holds meetings, and explains why change is needed.

This creates a more open, trusting organizational culture. The innovative-style leader tends to focus on technical matters and often overlooks the needs of people. The result is that there is typically resistance to change. The imaginative leader has a clear view of future needs and opportunities. However, because of the concern with future needs, current problems can sometimes be overlooked. In general, the imaginative leader also understands the needs of the organization and finds ways to include people in the vision. An inspirational leader, such as Richard Lewis, brings the organization along with his or her ideas. Thus, the creative styles of senior managers often determine whether change will be accepted at all. Customers, suppliers, government agencies, and the entire network that embraces our social and political structure must also accept innovation. For example, plasma is a gas used in super-thin, wide-screen televisions that provide excellent displays and are flicker-free. However, the price is extraordinarily high and customers may not see the added value of an exceptionally bright picture on a wide screen. This is an example of the difficulty of introducing a new product that has severe economic hurdles.

Over a period of time, even workers who are creative lose their motivation if they feel management is no longer interested in them. At Ore-Ida, the J. J. Heinz Co. producer of frozen potatoes, there was limited new product development even though innovation had been a strategic priority for years. The research department at Ore-Ida did not believe that management was serious about new product development. Shortly after managers shared their thinking with the research group, there were positive results. A million dollars in cost savings was uncovered in one year, and over a three-year period, there were numerous new products and product line extensions.

In many instances, it is not the sheer effort or willingness to be creative that assures results. Perseverance and patience are the qualities required for breakthrough achievements. Consider Edison's many experiments to find a filament for his light bulb, or Darwin spending years traveling around the globe gathering evidence for what became his Theory of Evolution. Most organizations don't have the time or resources to pursue long-term, complex projects. A company that was ahead of the curve in the development of a computer program that could transmit motion pictures over ordinary telephone lines had to give it up because of the complexity of inventing a new approach and the need for very talented workers. Resources were not available to complete the program in a reasonable period of time. As Amabile, Hadley, and Kramer described it, creativity gets killed when it is under the gun.

How Change Is Introduced

Many of the old rules governing how to institute change will have to be thrown out. Slow, incremental change in bureaucratic structures no longer works in meeting rapidly changing environmental crises. **A quantum leap is needed to deal with changing external forces.** Leaders will need to focus on opportunities along with productivity to achieve effective performance. Leaders who are concerned with significant change need to convince their organizations to accept new ideas. To accomplish this goal, language becomes an important aspect of portraying organizational vision. Using the right words is especially important when trying to convince employees to accept personal risk. This is more easily said than done. Gaining the confidence of employees is difficult. They will need to embrace a new culture, with new expectations. This requires sensitivity on the part of the leaders and must be backed up with credible behavior. Dealing with personal values and deeply held beliefs requires a leader who is sensitive to individual needs and is able to build confidence and gain commitment.

Bernard Denburg, an expert in turning troubled companies around, recognized the importance of empowering employees. He focused their efforts on innovation, not cost reduction, to turn sick companies around. Using this basic logic with over 45 troubled companies, he was able to make every one of them profitable. He recognized that the creative power of employees could work wonders. An example was the successful outcome at A&E PlastiPac, which used his strategy and their innovation to save the company. A&E produced plastic bags for food chains. When the large plastic manufacturers entered the field, they nearly drove A&E into bankruptcy. To counter this threat, Denburg challenged his staff to change the product so that it would be unique. With Denburg's help, they came up with the idea of adding the names of the food chains to the plastic bags and thereby A&E was able to recapture the market.

In his book *Leading the Revolution*, Gary Hamel maintains that in recent years, businesses have engaged in a technology race much like the international arms race. **In most cases, investments in technology have improved profits across the board. However, radical innovation is critical for companies to stay ahead of the pack. Fresh thinking and a passion for work are the key elements needed.** Hamel suggests that we recognize the need for innovative upheaval on the job rather than using incremental change. Two individuals at IBM, a programmer named David Grossman and a staff executive named John Patrick, kept pushing the unpopular idea of the Internet to their superiors. They found a variety of innovative ways to demonstrate the potential power of the Web. They were finally able to gather a group of believers, including CEO Louis V. Gerstner Jr., which eventually made IBM a major player in the Internet world.

Hamel claims that only radical change will lead to innovation, and that revolution is needed to achieve the goal of reinvention. Business has experienced rapid and often disruptive change in markets and technology over the past decade, and companies will have to make fundamental changes—reinvent themselves—to survive and prosper. On the other hand, there are those who contend that revolutionary change may not be best for all organizations because it causes monumental stress and not all organizations would survive intact. Those organizations believe that effective change can best be accomplished through well-planned, incremental means. The best advice is: If the shoe fits, wear it!

Part of the problem in introducing innovation is that companies flip back and forth between change practices. The first is economic change, such as restructuring and downsizing. Then it is organizational change, which includes the enhancement of employee attitudes and skills. Beer and Nohria contend that 70% of change projects fail because companies don't use both of these approaches together in a consistent and well-integrated manner. They do not feel that the revolutionary approach, so often advocated in recent years, is the correct way to proceed. Obviously, because of the differences regarding how best to introduce change, there is no one best answer. Some industries are better suited to change because that is how they remain ahead of the pack. Companies in biotechnology, the computer field, and advertising are examples of where change is both needed and accepted. In other companies, such as farm products and transportation, evolutionary change is preferred.

An example of balancing risk with a potentially high payoff was tried at Ballard Power Systems. Geoffrey Ballad wanted someone with a fresh and creative perspective—with few preconceived notions—to help design fuel cells. He hired a chemistry professor, Keith Prater, to work on fuel cell technology, even though the professor had no prior experience in the field. Obviously, Professor Prater's innovative style was transferable from chemistry to fuel cells. Consequently, Ballard's gamble paid off. Given the opportunity and the challenge, Prater made important breakthroughs in the development of fuel cells, which now power many of the buses and cars we use.

Microsoft recognized that there had to be a balance between innovation and discipline, so it hired Robert Herbold, a management consultant, to handle the crisis caused by an informal, creative atmosphere that was not meeting revenue targets. During his seven years at Microsoft, he was able to assist in quadrupling revenue and achieving a seven-fold increase in profits, while at the same time reducing operating expenses from 51% to 40%. How did he accomplish this? He started by identifying products that would excite customers, and then introduced a creative, new approach to sales. He had to overcome the isolated fiefdoms that existed within Microsoft, and to form an integrated information system that would be used by all managers throughout the company. A key success factor was his ability to "explain" why particular changes were needed. However, gaining acceptance of the changes required the leadership of a CEO who was sensitive to the creative needs of the organization as well as meeting customer needs.

Organizational Change

Organizational change, in general, is an exceedingly difficult task. Every leader recognizes that organizations must continuously adapt to changes in the external environment. Nonetheless, the introduction of organizational change creates anxiety and fear. When a major adjustment is required because of some newly proposed reorganization, it can lead to high levels of "fight, flight, or freeze." **To introduce continuous change, such as that required in today's turbulent environment, leaders need to recognize the importance of motivation and the involvement of employees.**

An example of how effective leadership helped to keep innovation and entrepreneurial energy alive was the approach taken by CEO George Hatsopoulos of Thermo Electron Corporation. He allowed each new project to spin off as a separate company, with Thermo Electron as the majority stakeholder. While thought by some to be primarily an innovation in capital financing, he believed it provided a strong incentive to employees, while at the same time being helpful in bringing in funding. His approach has been an ongoing success.

On the other hand, companies can inadvertently discourage innovation. A new marketing director was hired to help in meeting fierce competition. The director had an imaginative Creative Intelligence style that was different from everyone else in the conservative, family-owned company. He came up with many creative ideas that challenged the status quo and made people uncomfortable. His fellow employees were excited and not threatened by his ideas. However, when he presented a new product line to senior management, it was rejected out of hand, leading to stifled creativity. This is a classic case that illustrates the conflict that exists between the need for innovation in a changing marketplace on the one hand, and tradition-bound corporate culture on the other.

The alternative to rigidity and tradition is an approach taken by Chris Bangle, Global Chief of Design for BMW in Munich, Germany. He sees himself as living at the intersection of art and commerce. He constantly looks for ways to produce the "ultimate driving machine," while at the same time looking to make a profit. He uses three key principles. His first goal is to protect the creative team from the rest of the company as much as possible. Second, he insists on protecting the creative process from time pressures that could disrupt the focus of the work. Third, he communicates continuously with the team and mediates creatively between the design and business sides of the company. He says that the constant quest to convince non-designers that a BMW, like a fine wine, cannot be hurried is a most difficult task. He has to appeal to a deeply held, nonverbal belief about BMW-ness. Designers have a sense of pride about the product that they share with everyone in the company. The designers view perfection as ephemeral, an almost spiritual quest. They realize that it is a goal that needs to be achieved in stages. Engineers, on the other hand, feel that perfection is measurable and should be done right.

While technological innovation may be the foundation for competitive advantage, if not accepted or properly implemented, the advantage disappears. To assure acceptance of radical change, leaders also need to rely on their Emotional Intelligence. Daniel Goleman describes five components of Emotional Intelligence that include the following: self-awareness, self-confidence, relating to others, being open to change, and knowing what motivates you to pursue difficult goals. **Leaders need to**

know that others have feelings, and they must be persuasive in getting change accepted. Goleman describes how Emotional Intelligence is used to gain cooperation and encourage others to embrace high levels of innovation and creativity. Bangle often has to translate the language of art into a form that can be understood by the rest of the corporation. In persuading people to focus on the relevant aspects of creative design, he applies techniques such as keeping things concrete by speaking in descriptive, amusing terms, comparing design features to animals and people (a rear bumper sagging like a baby with a full diaper). He also uses pictures as much as possible to illustrate his points.

From another perspective, intrinsic motivation is also crucial for individuals who have a sense of personal purpose and who tend to devote their energy to the creative process. Extrinsic motivation includes public recognition, promotions, and tangible rewards. A study conducted at Pillsbury showed that brand managers valued rewarding both intrinsic and extrinsic motivation to stimulate innovation and creativity.

How can Creative Intelligence be used effectively in an organization? Using the following steps, any organization can increase its creativity quotient, that is, the ratio of available talent to that used:

- Start with identifying each individual's Creative Intelligence. An organization should strive to match abilities with requirements. Placing people in positions that utilize their abilities achieves better performance and more satisfied employees.

- Allow greater flexibility in positions within an organization. Creative people easily become bored. By providing rotation and new or challenging positions, management is able to retain valuable employees.

- Allow greater use of teamwork and recognize accomplishment. Although creative individuals have high levels of personal satisfaction in what they do, they also enjoy recognition by others of their accomplishments.

- Make the organization more flexible by introducing training that expands the horizons of the employees rather than emphasizes increased proficiency on the job.

- Encourage an "open" organization, where questioning and differences are accepted and respected. The creative mind thoroughly dislikes "limits" or having to adhere to the "party line."

- Most important, recognize that a small investment in individuals often has tremendous payback. Papermate had a major problem with leaking ballpoint pens. A young engineer volunteered to study quality control and reduced the rejected pens from 17% to 4%. This was a win-win solution. The engineer was thrilled at making that significant a contribution and Papermate saved its pen business.

Creativity and Organizational Culture

William C. Miller, President of Global Creativity Corporation, is concerned with fostering creativity. He considers Theresa Amabile's assertions about the failure of stretch goals to be very important. Amabile describes how a culture that emphasizes performance evaluation creates a climate of fear and an unwillingness to take risks. **Organizations cannot convince their best people to take personal risks if it entails a possible cost to their careers.** The answer is clear: People are not willing to expose themselves to being chastised for being different. Successful organizations have recognized that they need to tolerate differences among employees.

Organizational culture has a direct impact on how creativity and innovation are received. This is especially important where the underlying feelings and beliefs of a group go counter to those of creative individuals. The concept of organizational culture emphasizes shared, unspoken understanding in the minds of the organization's members. One example of the power of shared values was the phenomenal success of the Ford Taurus, where a change in focus emphasized quality as the top priority and led to radical changes. A new approach was used for the design of the cars: the Planning, Engineering, Design, and Manufacturing divisions acted together as the team that took final responsibility for the cars. The result was an outstanding success.

Organizational culture also reflects the basic assumptions and preferences that guide individual behavior. Culture links both the tangible and intangible factors reflecting these shared values. In addition, shared values often determine the degree of commitment that individuals are willing to make to the goals of the organization. **To obtain a commitment to innovation and creativity, leaders need to recognize that an individual's values and the organization's cultural norms must be compatible.** Or, stated differently, successful implementation requires that people be willing to change when required.

A major challenge facing leaders is how to reconcile individual values with cultural norms. One approach that has been highly successful in gaining commitment on the part of an individual is to provide the person the freedom to explore his or her own ideas. Where this approach has been used, unusual results have been achieved. A case in point was the development of the first IBM personal computer. By allowing a team in Boca Raton, Florida complete freedom, unfettered by the usual corporate constraints, it was able to leapfrog the competition and bring out one of the first personal computers.

John Akers, who was President of IBM, on the other hand, was a captive of IBM's traditionally rigid environment and wound up leaving the company because of his failure to turn it around. His successor, Lou Gerstner, came with an open mind and the mission of reinventing IBM. He devised an agile corporation that could leapfrog past its competition, and encouraged radical rather than incremental change. However, even Gerstner ran into problems when he tried to coerce Jim Manzi, a true entrepreneur, into taking a backseat. Manzi was known for being "strong-willed," sometimes abrasive, and generally a loner. He could not work for anyone; he wanted to be his own boss, and he ultimately left IBM.

Intrinsic motivation and creative performance are very often influenced by the way in which jobs are structured. Complex and demanding jobs generally foster greater motivation than simple and routine jobs. Individuals with high intrinsic involvement in their work are likely to be more focused, persistent, and open to alternatives that lead to greater creative potential. In addition to the structure of individual jobs, organizational systems are needed to support and encourage creative effort. Organizational environments that are most conducive to creative activity on the part of their employees have open communication between levels of the organization, encourage employee input into decisions, and allow considerable flexibility. Where there is a lack of organizational support coupled with rigid controls, employees often become discouraged and are unwilling to take the unusual risks that creativity demands.

Creativity at Work

In his study of organizations that foster innovation and creativity, Robert Sutton found that the most creative ones are also the least efficient, least organized, and often the least pleasant places in which to work. **Some managers find it difficult to support innovation and creativity, partly because their primary focus is on performance and any change could be disruptive.** As an example, Sutton describes how Gary Starkweather at Xerox invented the laser printer but was confronted with the problem of introducing change. Despite enormous resistance from Xerox managers and fellow researchers, Starkweather complained to senior management about how his idea and career were being ruined by "laboratory dogma." To correct the situation, Starkweather was transferred to the research facility in Palo Alto, California.

The result was that he was able to perfect the Xerox 9700 laser printer, which was introduced to the market and became a best-selling product.

Sutton describes **"successful heretics" as ones who believe passionately in what they envision, and are often very good at convincing others to buy into their ideas.** Apple cofounder Steve Jobs has what he calls his "reality distortion field," in which he convinces those around him to suspend disbelief and give him their full commitment. Burt Rutan did something similar with the development team for the Voyager aircraft that can fly around the globe without refueling. Rutan's edict to his engineers was to have confidence in nonsense because any idea might be the answer. Creative ideas come from the most persuasive and committed people. They have the best chance of success.

Introducing creativity into an organization generates many problems because of the reluctance to accept change. Creative individuals follow their own compass and can drive their colleagues and managers crazy. However, they can also push their companies into making winning gambles that they would never have made on their own. Richard Drew directly defied 3M's CEO, William McKnight, to continue work on what became masking tape. His work also made key contributions to Scotch tape. At Hewlett-Packard (HP), engineer Chuck House was ordered by David Packard to stop work on a display monitor that was deemed unsuccessful. House believed so strongly in the monitor that he used his own vacation time to show the prototype to potential customers. He was able to convince HP to put it into production, and it ended up producing $35 million in revenue for the company. David Packard later gave House a medal for having extraordinary contempt and defiance beyond the normal expectation of an engineer's duty.

"Innovation" is becoming a key word in today's competitive world. Microsoft and Merck have both been successful at hiring talented people who are pathfinders and who are good at improvising. Jack Welch at GE set up 60 independent ventures designed to teach people to be entrepreneurial. He recognized, however, that some of the 60 would fail. When General Motors (GM) first went into business, it was innovative and offered cars in a choice of colors at a time when the Ford Motor Company only offered cars in black. GM also introduced an innovation in financing that allowed people to buy cars without having cash in hand.

The Importance of Creative Individuals

Individuals, not organizations, are generally responsible for the innovations that bring about change. Geniuses, with their flashes of insight, imagination, and Creative Intelligence help move society forward. Unfortunately, geniuses in the arts and sciences can be very difficult to work with. They have fierce individuality and are impatient with those they see as less capable. Their egos are surprisingly fragile, making them emotionally vulnerable. However, organizations need to learn how to work effectively with geniuses if they want to compete effectively in the future.

Mark Morris, a choreographer and creative genius, constantly thinks and works at high speed. Impatient with those who can't keep up, he often hurts other dancers' feelings. He is described as being very bossy. In his role as the head of a dance company, he is faced with managing and directing other geniuses. He hates mentoring, but is willing to help dancers with their careers. He believes that inner motivation is critical. His business partners do the firing of employees who can't make it. Above all, he feels that he cannot tell a big star what to do. On the other hand, artists and geniuses appreciate the truth about themselves. They totally dislike false praise and meaningless encouragement. They do, however, look for recognition of their accomplishments.

Intellectual capability, along with creativity, determine a nation's or a corporation's potential. Intellect consists of factual knowledge, expert skills, and creativity. However, self-motivation is needed to assure that intellect is utilized. Another consideration is that motivated individuals who are creative are significantly more important than employees who rely on factual knowledge. Nonetheless, most companies still spend more money on basic training that emphasizes factual knowledge than on stimulating creativity. Those companies that encourage intellectual pursuits are able to exploit the exponential value of new knowledge. Knowledge and intellect grow where they are encouraged. **Innovative thinking attracts other talent that further stimulates creativity and enhances the ability to compete.** Think tanks, such as the Rand Corporation, at one time had the largest number of outstanding thinkers in the country, many of whom were Nobel Prize winners. This is an example of where intellectual individuals were attracted to an organization that encouraged creativity.

One way of achieving the best possible output from the intellectual members of an organization is to reduce mindless tasks and bureaucratic paperwork. Another is to eliminate the infighting that can occur because of rigid structures and formal rules. Manufacturing jobs have rarely been able to tap into the creative potential of workers. After doing the same task hundreds of times a day, there is little initiative for considering change in the workplace. Rather, the creative outlets for these workers are typically the hobbies or projects they pursue at home. Changes in the workplace and task requirements are needed to encourage creativity on the job. Typically, Japan has rewarded suggestions that have been adopted. The U.S., for the most part, does not consider suggestions as being important, which has led to low interest on the part of employees.

Creative individuals consider recognition for their contributions very important. An example is Kary Mullis, who was a chemist at Cetus, a small biotechnology company. He described how an idea came to him on how to achieve polymerase chain reaction (PCR) for quickly growing batches of DNA from mere fragments as he was driving his car. However, it was problematic to make the idea work in the laboratory. He worked alone on it unsuccessfully for three months. Cetus was becoming impatient and recommended that Mullis work on the problem with three of his colleagues. Their joint effort was eventually successful. In many cases, the experimental phase of getting an idea to work is as important as the original idea. Mullis, however, felt that he had been robbed by Cetus of the credit due him and eventually left the company. However, in 1993, Mullis received the Nobel Prize for the discovery of PCR. He felt that his role in discovering PCR was finally vindicated.

The world generally recognizes the value of a first discovery, though at times, credit is spread among those who independently came to the same conclusions. An example is Leibnitz and Newton and the discovery of calculus. Although Leibnitz published his book on calculus first, Newton had been working with the basic concepts for about 10 years prior to publishing his results.

How Creative People Behave

Paul MacCready, founder of AeroVironment, recognized that he had a restless mind that was always darting around. The American Society of Mechanical Engineers, however, named MacCready the Engineer of the Century for creating the world's first man-powered and solar-powered aircraft. He never stops coming up with innovative ideas, and he hires creative teams to carry them out. When discussing his innovative productivity, he plays down his abilities, but admits that he's especially good at synthesizing concepts and making connections. He says daydreaming is particularly productive and he has had some of his best ideas while on vacation.

Bill Gross is another example of a uniquely creative individual. Ben Rosen, co-founder of Compaq, described Gross as an extraordinary entrepreneur, a terrible manager, and a tragic figure of the Internet bust. His brain really sets him apart. He speaks fast and bubbles over with ideas and optimism. Together with his overpowering intellect, he has a personal charisma that entices people to follow him and buy into his visions. It seems as though ideas just pour out of him with each being more original than the previous one and each having genuine promise.

Many business leaders talk about creativity and innovation, but few believe their companies are doing a good job fostering either one. Dr. Stanley S. Gryskiewicz, who has studied organizations for 25 years, says that innovation requires both creativity and implementation of new ideas. He found that some organizational structures are better at supporting innovation and creativity than others. The ones that were considered innovative had to be consciously designed to encourage creativity. He suggests that innovation and creativity involve positive turbulence. This is not chaos, but rather turmoil that provides the stimulation needed to encourage change. Organizations that make a commitment to supporting creativity will need to budget sufficient resources to carry it out, and they will need to consider both the individual's and organization's needs. Companies such as Nortel Network's Broadband division committed 10–15% of their budgets at quarterly management meetings to obtaining new ideas from the outside world.

Dr. Alim Louis Benabid, a French neurosurgeon researching treatments for Parkinson's disease, came up with the idea of electrical stimulation of the brain to control tremors. He used electrodes during surgery to stimulate and identify specific parts of the brain needed to correct the disease. This gave him the idea of using electrical stimulation for long-term ailments, not just as a diagnostic tool. He worked with Medtronic, a Minneapolis-based maker of medical electrode devices. With their collaboration, he developed Aptiva, a safe device approved by the FDA in 1997. The success was attributed to Medtronic because it was "safe" to take this kind of innovative risk. This electrode treatment shows great promise. Drugs are only effective for a few years for Parkinson's patients, and often have unpleasant side effects. Electrodes have the advantage of affecting only the precise spot where they're needed in the brain. Scientists are now looking at other possible uses for deep-brain stimulation, such as for treating epilepsy and possibly some psychiatric disorders.

Applying Creativity

Advances in biotechnology have contributed significantly to improving the health and saving the lives of people with chronic illnesses. Researchers have found that copying the way our bodies fight disease can cure many problems for which we currently have no effective treatment. Monoclonal antibodies are now genetically engineered to find and destroy cancers and other foreign bodies. Synthetic antibodies are also being tried as a way of treating certain diseases. Additionally, vaccines that target cancers of the brain, breast, ovaries, prostate, and other parts of the body are being tested. Imagine the impact that biotechnology can have on our health because of innovative research conducted by dedicated people. Other advances in understanding the genetic functions of plants and animals can significantly contribute to important needs of society. Plants have provided many of the chemicals used for pharmaceuticals, and now the possibility of using plants as a renewable source of energy is being explored.

These technological advances portend radical changes in society, lifestyles, health, longevity, and the way in which our brains function. Science is working on decoding the fundamental rules of nature. Furthermore, **scientific discovery is moving at an ever-increasing pace, both because of tools such as super-computers and the growth of knowledge regarding the fundamental laws that govern almost every aspect of life.**

One significant change that is being pursued is the availability of abundant forms of energy that can sustain continued growth while maintaining or increasing our standard of living. To some extent, advances in science contribute to leaps in creativity that can lead to unprecedented changes in our political and social systems. Considering the extent of major scientific breakthroughs, one that stands out is the computer, which will become ubiquitous as it is imbedded in "intelligent" devices. Computers potentially will have a significant impact on education, the transmission of medical information, military operations, and the distribution of wealth, agriculture, and more. All portend important advances, but also significant challenges, including the impact on human behavior and the greater need to both understand creativity and employ it in a positive way. Chip implants are being tested for blind spots in the eye, relieve deafness, and stimulate our ability to mentally process information using icons and other "visual" constructs that convey "meaning" rather than "data."

Michio Kaku describes three basic scientific advances that will change civilization as we know it. First is quantum theory, which states that energy is not continuous, but rather comprised of energy bundles called "quanta." An example is the photon, which defines a quantum or packet of light and follows well-defined laws that allow us to form new kinds of basic materials. The second advance is the information revolution spawned by the computer. As more transistors are placed on microchips, whole new dimensions will evolve because of the ability to add intelligence to information via the Internet. Changes in lifestyles and medicine resulting from computer applications will dramatically affect the quality of life. The third revolution, bio-molecular technology, is revealing the details of DNA, including how atoms bond and the DNA code for all living organisms such as viruses and bacteria.

In *Intelligent Information Systems*, Rowe and Davis describe how to match the phenomenal capability of the computer with the cumbersome processing of information by human managers. Recent advances in computer programs such as SAP and Peoplesoft are beginning to integrate the information needs of managers and others in organizations. Even business strategy will be made by computer because of the rapid changes that are taking place.

Smart cards are now being used to store and transmit information. Smart cars are emerging that can help drivers sense and avert dangers. Displays help motorists find the best route to a desired destination. Virtual reality is being used to transform physical objects into computer code that allows manipulation of the design or can improve the sales potential of home products.

According to Kaku, bionics are moving toward harnessing the remarkable speed of quantum transistors to interface directly with neurons in the brain. Doctors at Harvard Medical School are working on a bionic eye that will use implanted chips to restore vision. Scientists predict that using computer chips could reactivate a number of paralyzed body organs. Quantum cryptography will be used to develop unbreakable computer codes. Jobs that can be done on the Internet will eliminate scores of routine tasks. Finally, increasingly "intelligent" robots will be able to carry out many functions without human intervention.

The Futurist, a publication of the World Future Society, describes the projected changes and trends for the next 25 years. Can we really forecast the future, and if so, with what accuracy? Forecasts, in many instances, are extensions of what we know today. But what about creativity and the ability to see what no one else sees? Can radical departures be predicted? In the late 1800s, it was suggested that the U.S. Patent Office be closed because everything had been invented that could be! With knowledge growing exponentially, who can say what the future holds? Nonetheless, we can "conjecture" about what experts in various fields believe will be coming and that will have a profound impact on all our lives.

In their Special Report, *Forecasts for the Next 25 Years*, the World Future Society forecasts a number of changes. For example, the group forecasts that the 80 million people born between 1977 and 1997 will have significantly more power than their parents dreamed possible. Within the next 25 years, we should be able to grow new organs, tissue, and cartilage. To root out terrorism, world powers will spend up to $9 billion per year to aid developing countries. Will this solve the problem or are value systems more critical in shaping people's behavior?

New technologies that are forecast include: mapping the human genome, super-strength materials, new energy sources, smart manufacturing, anti-aging products, and many others. One of the most critical forecasts is that we will run out of water by 2040 for 3.5 billion people. Even using the polar ice cap for water will not suffice. A creative solution for water purification, such as using ocean water, could prevent this disastrous forecast.

Successful innovation seldom is based on a "flash of inspiration." Rather, it requires a disciplined pursuit of a desired outcome and knowing what to do to achieve objectives. There are numerous instances of brilliant ideas that eventually become successful products. Accidental or unexpected events can often trigger innovative change, such as the discovery of penicillin or X-rays. Bringing new ideas or products to fruition, however, requires considerable effort, including public acceptance, the ability to produce at an acceptable price, and finding new ways of distribution such as on the Internet. This is the case with almost every major advance that has been made. Computers and their applications, including robotics and artificial intelligence, have had a profound impact on the world and are becoming an integral part of every major product. From wristwatches to spacecraft, computers have made advances possible way beyond anything their inventors could have imagined.

Where is innovation today? A major advance beyond computers is information use and the Internet. Intel's silicon wafer will contribute to wireless, worldwide communication. Biomedicine will produce new drugs and diagnostic technology that can be tailored for the individual based on genetic makeup. This will lead to DNA chips that will be able to guide physicians in prescribing medication that takes into account the patient's blood pressure or other specific needs. The Massachusetts Institute of Technology is working on a biosensor to instantly determine a "point of care diagnosis."

Research is progressing on the extension of a biosensor chip that would determine how well enzymes are metabolizing drugs that are prescribed. Toxic effects or other reactions could be detected easily during a routine examination in the doctor's office.

Nano-technology will be able to provide a rapid, inexpensive capability to perform tasks previously considered impossible. Computers will be able to incorporate memory in each molecule to provide more efficient information storage. This in turn may lead to very sensitive devices, such as flat-panel screens or lasers that operate at super-speed. Computers would fit into any device that could benefit from their small size, including powerful devices such as airplane instruments, telephone transmission, automobile applications, and so on.

Medicine continues to make major advances, such as the recently announced method of surgery using high-frequency sound waves that focus in on and destroy cancer cells that are then absorbed by the body. The high-frequency device uses waves that are at a level that is too high for people to hear. Combined with the high-frequency waves are low-frequency sound waves that create three-dimensional images similar to ultrasound and show the physician what is happening inside the body. Imagine doing brain surgery without having to open the skull. The precision of the high-frequency sound waves has the potential of being better than the scalpel normally used by surgeons.

Another significant change is the design of "smart engines" that cruise along with minimal human intervention. Global positioning could become a standard feature on cars of the future. Flying airplanes is a tedious task that requires constant attention. New technology using ultra-smart, ultra-small computers could help pilots avoid airline crashes, and to find the best routes to travel to reduce time, energy, and effort. If all these technological marvels could be applied to the problems confronting us, what a wonderful world this could be!

The Future Is Now

Ten chairmen of the board and 32 company presidents were included in a research study done by the author. Each was interviewed regarding how they planned the future of their company. The sample included both large and small companies from a variety of industries. Some were entrepreneurs and others were single proprietors. The results were very informative in that they pointed out the differences among industries and different sized organizations. The findings were discussed individually with the executives who were concerned about planning the future of their organizations. Although this study cannot be extrapolated to all industries, it did emphasize a concern for creativity. Because of rapid change in technology and severe international competition, these leaders increasingly recognized the value of innovation. They increasingly accepted that creativity is not a discretionary item, but is an integral part of assuring the success and survival of their companies.

Those who dare to challenge the enormous problems we face are most likely to embrace creative solutions. Not only must we consider how to achieve effective organizational performance, but we also need to recognize the impact of the vast disparities in the way people live around the world. Creativity by itself does not change things. However, it offers the possibility of changing our world for the better.

Applying the Creative Potential Profile, we can improve organizational performance by appropriately using the following steps:

1. Start by recognizing that every individual is different and use the test instrument to better align talent with requirements.

2. Apply the test instrument to identify each individual's Creative Intelligence style.

3. When considering a restructuring or downsizing of an organization, apply the test instrument to match the requirements needed.

4. Recognize that each individual has different aspiration levels and find a way to accommodate these differences.

5. The current environment requires adaptability and flexibility, which often demand rapid response. The test instrument can be a valuable adjunct for knowing would would be best at making critical decisions.

6. Recognize the need for a learning organization that is continuously transforming as demands of the external environment change.

7. Apply the test instrument to establish teams by matching requirements with available talent.

Applying the Creative Potential Profile will increasingly become a requirement to meet the ever-changing demands on an organization.

General Eisenhower, who was an extraordinary leader, recognized that people who value privilege above principle wind up losing both. His words of wisdom can be applied to creativity. We have a choice. Will we use our vast talents to make our lives better or will we miss the opportunity to bring about significant change?

What have you learned after reading this book? You should have a better idea of what creativity entails, how difficult it can be to introduce creativity into an organization, including education, and the need for great leaders to assure that we embrace creativity. By examining the lives of the many people covered in the book, you should have a better understanding of who creative people are, what they do, how they behave, and what makes them successful. Most important, you should recognize the significance of creativity in every aspect of our lives. To fully appreciate the role of creativity, you should examine your Creative Potential Profile and determine your Creative Intelligence styles to have a better understanding of who you are, what you can do, and how you can be creative about your own future.

BIBLIOGRAPHY

"A Creative Dialogue," *Psychology Today.* (July/August, 1999), pp. 58-61.

Acton, G. S. and Schroeder, D. H. "Sensory Discrimination as Related to General Intelligence." *Intelligence.* (29, 2001), 263 – 271.

Adams, Susan. "What Is Genius Made Of?" *Forbes.* November 13, 2000, p. 404.

Albert, R. S., editor, *Genius and Eminence: The Social Psychology of Creativity and Exceptional Achievement.* Oxford, England: Pergamon Press, 1983.

Allman, William F. "The Dawn of Creativity." *U.S. News and World Report.* May 20, 1996, pp. 53-58.

Allman, William F. "Why IQ Isn't Destiny." *U. S. News & World Report.* October 24, 1994, pp. 73-80.

Amabile, Teresa M. Constance N. Hadley, and Steven J. Kramer. "Creativity Under the Gun." *Harvard Business Review,* August, 2002, pp. 52-61.

Amabile, Teresa M. *Growing Up Creative*. Buffalo: *C.E.F. Press*, 1989,

Anderson, John. *The Architecture of Cognition*. Cambridge, Massachusetts: Harvard University Press, 1983.

Anderson, Joseph V. "Weirder than Fiction: the Reality and Myths of Creativity." *Academy of Management Executive*, Vol. 6 No. 4, 1992, pp. 40-47.

Baldwin, Neil. "The Lesser Known Edison." *Scientific American*, February, 1997, pp. 62-67.

Bangle, Chris. "How BMW Turns Art into Profit." *Harvard Business Review,* January, 2001, pp. 47-55.

Barletta, Ralph. "An Introduction to Case-Based Reasoning." *A.I. Expert*, August, 1991, pp. 43-49.

Barron, Frank, Alfonso Montuori, and Anthea Barron. (editors), *Creators on Creating,* Cambridge: G. P. Putnam, 1997.

Barron, Frank. *Creativity and Psychological Health*. Princeton, N.J.: Van Nostrand, 1963.

Barsalou, L. W. *Deriving Categories to Achieve Goals*. In G. H. Bower (Ed.), The *Psychology of Learning and Motivation: Advances in Research and Theory,* Vol. 27, 1-64. New York: Academic Press, 1991.

Barsalou, L. W. "Ad hoc Categories." *Memory & Cognition,* October, 1983, pp. 211-227.

Barsalou, L. W. *The Instability of Graded Structure: Implications for the Nature of Concepts*. In U. Neisser (Ed.), *Concepts and Conceptual Development: Ecological and Intellectual Factors in Categorization,*Cambridge: Cambridge University Press, 1987.

Basala, G. *The Evolution of Technology*. Cambridge: Cambridge University Press, 1988.

Basden, Jonathan C. "Authentic Tasks as the Basis for Multimedia Design Curriculum." *T.H.E. Journal*, November, 2001, pp.16-21.

Beer, Michael and Nohria, Nitin. "Change Is Changing," *Harvard Business Review,* April, 2001, p. 125.

Begley, Sharon. "The Stuff That Dreams Are Made Of." *Newsweek*, August 14, 1989, pp.41- 44.

Begley, Sharon. Wright, L., Church, L., Hagar, M. "Mind Mapping." *Fortune,* April,1992, pp. 119-124.

Bennis, Warren and Robert J. Thomas. "Crucible of Leadership." *Harvard Business Review at Large*, September, 2002, pp. 39-45.

Bernstein, Aaron. Grounded: *Frank Lorenzo and the Destruction of Eastern Airlines*, Maryland:Beard Books, 1999.

Bhannick, Subir. "What's Mother Teressa Got to do with it?" *Time magazine,* October 21, 2002, p. 8.

Bickman,Martin. *Uncommon Learning: Henry David Thoreau*, New York: Norton Publishers, 1999.

Boden, Margaret A. "Précis of The Creative Mind: Myths and Mechanisms." *Behavioral and Brain Sciences* 17-3, 1994, pp. 519-570.

Bodnar, Janet. "Those Who Can, Teach." *Kiplinger's,* March, 2002, pp. 94-96.

Boorstin, Daniel J. *The Creators*. New York: Random House. 1992.

Boorstin, Daniel J. *The Discovers*. New York: Random House. 1983.

Bransford, J. D. and B.S. Stein, *The Ideal Problem Solver.* New York: Freeman. 1984.

Breyer, Christopher. "Richard Feynman and Guessing and Testing: The Art of Science". *Performing Arts,* May 13, 2001, pp. 8-12.

Brickhouse, Thomas and Nicholas Smith. *Plato's Socrates*. Oxford: Oxford University Press, 1994.

Brimelow, Peter. "Are Universities Necessary?", *Forbes,* April 26 ,1993, pp. 170-171.

Brimelow, Peter. "Too Much Homework?", *Forbes,* December 25, 2000, p. 108.

Bronowski, J. *The Ascent of Man.* Boston: Little, Brown and Company, 1973.

Brooker, Katrina. "The Chairman of Board Looks Back," *Fortune,* May 28, 2001, pp. 63-76.

Brophy, Beth and Erica E. Goode. "Amazing Families," *U.S. News & World Report,* December 12, 1988, pp. 78-87.

Brown, R., and Herrnstein, R. *Psychology.* Boston: Little, Brown. 1976.

Brownlee, Shannon and Traci Watson. "The Senses," *U.S. News and World Report* January 13, 1997, pp. 51-59.

Burke, Lisa A. and Monica K. Miller. "Taking the Mystery out of Intuitive Decision Making," *Academy of Management Executive,* (Vol. 13, No. 4, 1999), pp. 91-98.

Burrows, Peter and William Echikson. "HP's Woes are Deeper Than Downturn," *Business Week*, May 7, 2001, p.48.

Business Week. "100 years of Innovation," Special Issue, Summer 1999.

Buzan, Tony and Barry Buzan. *How to Use Radiant Thinking to Maximize Your Brain's Untapped Potential,* 2003. The Mind Map Book.

Cacciari, C., Levorato, M. C., and P. Cicogna. "Imagination at Work: Conceptual and Linguistic Creativity in Children." *In* T. B. Ward, S. M. Smith, & J. Vaid (Eds.). "Creative Thought: An Investigation of Conceptual Structures and Processes," Washington, DC:, *American Psychological Association*, 1997, pp. 145-177.

Calverley, Bob. "USC Chemists Teach Better Through Web Chemistry". *The University of Southern California Chronicle,* 2003.

Carlson, John G. and Alan J. Rowe. "How much does forgetting cost?" *Industrial Engineering Journal,* September, 1976, pp. 40-47.

Carter, Rita. *Mapping the Mind.* Berkeley and Los Angeles: University of California Press. 1998.

Cattell, R. B. *Abilities: Their Structure, Growth and Action.* Boston: Houghton Mifflin. 1971.

Chalmers, David J. "The Puzzle of Conscious Experience." *Scientific American* December, 1995, pp. 80-86.

"Change is Changing." *Harvard Business Review,* April, 2001, p. 125.

Childre, Doc and Howard Martin. "The HeartMath Solution."San Francisco: *Harper.* 1999.

Chinn, Clark A. and William F. Brewer. "The Role of Anomalous Data in Knowldge Acquisition: A Theoretical Framework and Implications for Science Instruction." *Review of Educational Research,* Spring,Vol. 63, No. 1, 1993, pp. 1-49.

Chomsky, N. *Language and Mind.* New York: Harcourt, Brace, Jovanovich. 1972.

Clapham, Maria M. "Employee Creativity: The Role of Leadership." *Academy of Management Executive,* August, 2000, pp. 138-139.

Clottes, Jean. "France's Magical Cave Art", *National Geographic,* Vol. 200, No. 2, 2001, p. 104.

COGITO. "The Modern History of Intelligence." *The University of Queensland ,* Australia, 1995.

Cohen, Gene D. "c =meΣ", *Modern Maturity,* March-April, 2000, pp. 30-35.

Colvin, Richard Lee. "Crusader Argues School Reforms Hinder Learning," *Los Angeles Times,* February 22, 2000, pp. A1 and A15.

Cone, Dick. "Psychology 499: Students Apply Theory to Real World," *USC Chronicle,* 1999, pp. 1-6.

Cornish, Edward. "Forecast for the Next 25 Year," *World Future Society-Futurist*, 2003, pp. 3-15.

Coy, Peter. "The Mother of Invention? Freedom," *Business Week*, May 2, 1994, p. 12.

Creative Productivity. In R. J. Sternberg & J. E. Davidson (Eds.), *Conceptions of Giftedness,* Cambridge: Cambridge University Press, 1986.

Crick, Francis and Christof Koch. "Why Neuroscience May Be Able to Explain Consciousness." *Scientific America,* December 1995, pp.84 -85.

Crovitz, H. F. *Galton's Walk: Methods for the Analysis of Thinking, Intelligence, and Creativity,* New York: Harper & Row. 1976.

Csikszentmihalyi, M. *Creativity: Flow and the Psychology of Discovery and Invention.* New York: Harper Collins, 1996.

Csikzentmihalyi, Mihaly and Robert Epstien. "A Creative Dialogue," *Psychology Today,* July-August, 1999, pp. 58-61.

Dacey, John S. and Kathleen H. Lennon. *Understanding Creativity*, San Francisco: Jossey-Bass, 1998.

Dahle, Cheryl. "Have You Seen the Five Faces of Genius?" *Fast Company,* October, 2000, pp. 84-86.

Damasio, Antonio R. "Thinking and Feeling." *Scientific American,* June 1997, pp. 140-1.

Damasio, Antonio R. and Hanna Damasio. "Brain and Language." *Scientific American,* September 1992, 89-95.

Day, Laura. "Laura Day Tells How to Develop Your Intuition." *Bottom Line.* February 1, 1997, pp. 11-12.

De Bono, Edward. "Master Thinkers Handbook," *International Center for Creative Thinking,* November 27, 2000, pp. 161-180.

De Treville, Susan. "Improving the Innovation Process," *OR/MS Today*, December, 1994, pp. 8-30.

DeBono, Edward. "Future Positive," February 26-29, 1980, *Seminar brochure: AMR International Inc.*

Denardo, Eric V. "The Science of Decision-Making," *OR/MS Today,* August, 2001, pp. 30-32.

Dervin, D. Creativity and Culture: *A Psychoanalyic Study of the Creative Process in the Arts, Sciences and Culture*. Cranbury, N. J.: Fairleigh Dickenson University Press.

DiPaolo, Andy. "Stanford Learning: Worldwide Availability On - Demand at Stanford Online." *T.H.E. Journal,* December, 1999, pp. 16-18.

"Does Class Size Matter?" *Scientific American,* November 2001, pp.79-85.

Donaldson, S. R. *The Real Story,* New York: Bantam Press, 1992.

Dooley, Ken, Editor. "Good Stuff: Collection of Insights & Inspiration." *Progressive Business Publications.* 2000, p. 15.

Drelicharz, Joseph A. "The Stem of Most Learning—I Wonder." *Program Manager*, July-August, 1995, pp. 8-10.

Drucker, Peter F. "The State of Innovation." *Technology Review*, June, 2002, pp. 55-63.

Drucker, Peter F. "The Discipline of Innovation, The Innovative Enterprise," *Harvard Business Review,* August 2002, pp. 95-102.

Drucker, Peter. "The Power of Innovation," *Inc,* May 29, 2000, pp. 103-104.

Drucker, Peter, F. "Putting More Now Into Knowledge," *Forbes,* May 15 2001, pp. 84-94.

Dunn, Samantha. "You Say You Want a Revolution?" *UCLA Magazine,* Winter, 1993, pp. 25-28.

Dwight D. Eisenhower. "Values vs. Privileges," *Kansas Heritage Server*, January, 1953.

Editors, Time-Life Books. *Secrets of the Inner Mind.* Alexandria, VA: Time-Life Books. 1993

Ehrenberg, Ronald G., Dominic J. Brewer, Adam Gamoran and J. Douglas Willms. Englewood Cliffs, New Jersey. 1998.

Erlbaum, Ochse, R. *Before the Gates of Excellence*. Cambridge: Cambridge University Press. 1990.

Feist, Gregory. The Influence of Personality on Artistic and Scientific Creativity in R. Ferra, Bartolome, Chopin and George Sand in Majorca, M.S.G. Haskell House, 1974.

Feynman, Richard P. *Surely You're Joking, Mr. Feynman,* W.W. Norton & Co., New York: London, 1985.

Finke, R. A. Creative *Imagery: Discoveries and Inventions in Visualization*. Hillsdale, N. J.: Eribaum, 1990.

Finke, R. A., Ward, T. B., & Smith, S. M. *Creative Cognition: Theory, Research, and Applications*. Cambridge, Mass.: MIT Press, 1992.

Fischbach, Gerald D. "Mind and Brain." *Scientific American,* September, 1992, pp. 48-57.

Fitzgerald, F. Scott "The Crack-up," New York: *New Directions*. 1945.

Fletcher, Geoffrey. "Education Act Sets Stage for Technology Reform," *T.H.E. Journal* February, 2002, p. 56.

Frohman, Mark and Perry Pascarella. "Achieving Purpose, Drive, and Innovation." *Industry Week,* March, 1990, pp.20-25.

Gardner, H. "Seven Creators of the Modern Era." *In* J. Brockman (Ed.), *Creativity,* New York: *Simon & Schuster,* 1993, pp.28- 47.

Gardner, H. *Creating Minds*. New York: Basic Books. 1993.

Gardner, H. *Frames of Mind: The Theory of Multiple Intelligences*. New York: Basic Books, 1993.

Gardner, H. *To Open Minds,* New York: Basic Books, 1989.

Gardner, Walt. "Why I Retired Early From Teaching in L.A.", *The Wall Street Journal,* December 17, 1992, op ed.

Gardner, Walt,."Do All These Tests Help Students?" Letters to the editor, *Los Angeles Times,* March 17, 2002.

Garrison Jessica. "The Irresistible Force of a Teacher's Will." *L.A. Times,* April, 2002, p. A29.

Geier, John G. and Dorothy E. Downey. *Energitics of Personality.* Minneapolis, MN, Aristos Publishing House. 1989.

Gentner, D., Brem, S., Ferguson, R., Wolff, P., Markham, A. B., & Forbus, K., "Analogy and Creativity in the works of Johannes Keplar." In T. B. Ward, S. M. Smith and J. Vaid (Eds) "Creative Thought: An Investigation of Conceptual Structures and Processes," Washington D.C., *American Psychological Association* 1997, pp. 403-459.

Gerstner, Louis V. Jr. "The Tests We Know We Need." Responses to an Op-Ed article March 14, 2002, *Los Angeles Times.*

Getzels, J. W., & Csikszentmihalyi, M. *The Creative Artist as an Explorer,* In J. McVicker Hunt (Ed.), *Human Intelligence,* New Brunswick, NJ: Transaction Books, 1972. pp. 182-192.

Getzels, J. W., & Csikszentmihalyi, M. *The Creative Vision: A Longitudinal Study of Problem Finding in Art.* New York: *Wiley,* 1976.

Getzels, J. W., and Jackson, P. W. *Creativity and Intelligence. Explorations with Gifted Students,* New York: *Wiley.* 1962.

Glass, Arnold Lewis, Keith James Holyoak and John Lester Santa. *Cognition.* Reading MA: Addison-Wesley Publishing Company, 1979. Golden, Frederic, "Leonardo Redux," Dec. 9, *Time,* 1996, 13

Golden, Frederic. "The Worst and the Brightest," *Time,* Vol. 156, No. 16, Oct. 16, 2000.

Goldman-Rakic, Patricia S. "Working Memory and the Mind." *Scientific American,* September 1992, pp.111-117.

Goleman, Daniel."What Makes a Leader?", *Harvard Business Review,* November-December, 1998, pp.93-102.

Golomb, Solomon. "W. Claude E. Shannon :1916-2001." *Science,* Vol. 292, 20 April 2001. p. 455.

Greeno, James G. "A Perspective on Thinking," *American Psychologist*, Vol. 44, No. 2, February, 1989, pp. 134-141.

Grossman, John. "The Idea Guru," *INC. Magazine,* May 2001, pp. 32-41.

Gruber, H.E. *Darwin on Man: A Psychological Study of Scientific Creativity.*

Grudin, Robert. *The Grace of Great Things*, New York: Ticknor and Fields, 1990.

Gryskiewicz, Stanley S. "Cashing in On Creativity at Work," *Psychology Today,* October-November, 2000, 83pp.-85.

Guest, Edgar. *The Manager's Book of Quotations,* NY: American Management Associoation, 1989.

Guilford, J. P. *The Nature of Human Intelligence,* New York: McGraw Hill, 1967.

Hamel, Gary. "Leading the Revolution," *Harvard Business School*, Mass., 2000.

Hammer, M., and Champy, J. *Reengineering the Corporation.* New York: Harper Business, 1993.

Handy, Charles. *The Age of Unreason, -Reinventing Education*, Business Books, Ltd., Great Britain, 1989.

Hart, Leslie A. "Brain-Compatible Teaching." *Today's Education* November-December 1978, pp. 42-45.

Henry, Jane. *Creative Management,* London: The Open University, 1991.

Herrera, Stephan. "Lateral Thinking." *Forbes,* August 10,1998, pp. 108.

Hershman, D. J., and Lieb, J. *The Key to Genius,* Buffalo, NY: Prometheus, 1988.

Hickock, Gregory, Ursula Bellugi and Edward S. Klima. "Sign Language and the Brain." *Scientific American,* June, 2001, Vol. 284, No. 6.

Holstein, William J. "Rewiring the Brain," *U. S. News & World Report,* March 1, 1999, pp. 52-53.

Hotz, Robert Lee. "Deciphering the Miracles of the Mind." *Los Angeles Times,* October 13, 1996, pp. A1, A20-A22.

Houston, Paul D. and Diane Gingold. "Designing Learning Systems for the 21st Century," *Fortune,* May 13, 1996, in the "Special Advertising Section."

Huffstutter, P. J. and Robin Fields. "A Virtual Revolution in Teaching," *Los Angeles Times* March 3, 2000, p. A15.

Im, James. "Develops Computer on Glass," *Engineering News,* Spring 2001, pp. 1 -2.

James, Peter and Nick Thorpe. *Ancient Inventions*, Ballantine Books: New York, 1994.

Jaroff, Leon. "The Bird Watcher," *Time Magazine*, Vol. 156 December 4, 2000, pp.102.

Johnson, George. "Lots of Action in the Memory Game," *Time,* June 12, 2000, pp. 54-57.

Joseph Nagyvary. "Secrets of the Stradivarius," *Scientific America,* July 2, 2002, p. 12.

Kahalas, Harvey and Kathleen Suchon, "Managing a Perpetual Idea Machine: Inside the Creator's Mind," *Academy of Management Executive*, Vol. 9, No. 2, 1995, pp.57-66.

Kaku, Michio. *Visions*, Anchor Books, Doubleday, New York, London, 1997.

Kandel, Eric R. and Robert D. Hawkins. "The Biological Basis of Learning and Individuality," *Scientific American,* September, 1992, pp.79-86.

Kantrowitz, Barbara, Pat Wingert, Brendon Burns, Pia Hinckle, Ruth Marshall, Catherine S. Kearsley, G. *Explorations in Learning and Instruction: The Theory Into Practice Database,* JSU Encyclopedia of Psychology, 1994-2001.

Kartzman, Joel. "An Interview with Howard Gardner," Thought Leaders, *Harvard Business Review,* First quarter, 1999, pp. 90-99.

Kennedy, Michael J. "The Cult of Richard Feynman," *L.A. Times Magazine*, Dec. 2, 2001, pp. 16, 48-58.

Khurana, Rakesh. "The Curse of the Superstar CEO," *Harvard Business Review*, September, 2002, pp.60-66.

Kim, S.H. *Essence of Creativity.* New York, Oxford University Press, 1990.

Kindall, M.B. and Buckland, W.R. Dictionary of Statistical Terms. New York: Hafner Publishing Co., 1960.

Klein, Gary. *Intuition at Work*, New York, Doubleday Publishing, 2003.

Kluger, Jeffrey. "The Battle to Save Your Memory," *Time,* June 12, 2000, pp. 46-53.

Koestler, A. *The Act of Creation.* London: Hutchinson. 1964.

Konner, Melvin. interviewed by Alvin P. Sanoff. "The Legacy of Our Genes," *U. S. News & World Report,* January 14, 1991, p. 53.

Krahe, Barbara. *Personality and Social Psychology.* London:Sage Publications, 1992.

Krause, Thomas, R., John Hidley and R. Scott Stricoft. "How Hard Wired is Human Behavior?" *Harvard Business Review,* Nov-Dec. 1998, pp. 170-171.

Kwang, Min Jang. "Calling Attention to More Diverse Approaches to Intelligence. Response to Paik. "*Washington University*, 1998, pp. 6-7.

Labich, Kenneth, "What Our Kids Must Learn." *Fortune,* (January 27, 1990), 64-66.

LeDoux, Joseph. *Review of the Emotional Brain: The Mysterious Underpinnings of Emotional Life,* Simon & Schuster, New York, 1996.

Lee Hotz, Robert. Deciphering the Miracles of the Mind, Los Angeles Times, October 13, 1996, pp. 19-22.

Lee, Fiona. "The Fear Factor," *Harvard Business Review*, Jauary, 2001, pp. 29-30.

Lemonick, Michael D. "Smart Genes?" *Time,* September 13, 1999, pp. 54 -58.

Lerner, Preston Laureate. "Roulette." *Los Angeles Times Magazine* December 2, 2001, pp.42-44.

Lewis, Peter. "Plasma: It's a Gas," *Fortune,* July 8, 2002, pp. 154-156.

Locke, Gary A. "Vision for the 21st Century," *Crosstalk*, 1998, p. 14.

Logothetis, Nikos K. "Vision: A Window on Consciousness," *Scientific American,* November, 1999, pp. 68-75.

Lowery, Lawrence F. "Inquiry: The Emphasis of a Bold, New Science Curriculum." *Technological Horizons in Education,* March, 1994, pp. 50-52.

Malone, Michael S. "God, Stephen Wolfram, and Everything Else," *Forbes ASAP.*

Malone, Michael S. "The Smother of Invention," *Forbes ASAP,* June 24, 2002, pp. 32-40.

Manegold, Farai Chideya, Theresa Waldrop, Donna Foote and Daniel Pedersen. "The Best Schools in the World." *Newsweek*, 1991, pp. 50-64.

Mann, Richard. "Learning on the Internet," *USC Chronical,* May 15, 1996, pp. 2-5.

Marayama, Magoroh. "Mindscapes in Management," *Academy of Management Review*, Vol. 21, No. 2, 1996, pp. 558-579.

Marhes, Kathleen. "Wining the Ivory Tower," *Business Week*, August 9,1999, pp. 90-92.

Markova, Dawna. *Open Mind*, Berkley:Conari Press, 1996.

Marsa, Linda. "Doing Surgery Without Scalpels, but Sound Waves," *L.A. Times*, Oct. 28, 2002, p. F3.

Masie, Elliott. "New Thinking Needed to Alter Learner's Behavior," *Computer Reseller News,* August 17, 1998, pp. 47-49.

Mathews, Jay. "Escalante Still Stands and Delivers." *Newsweek,* July 20, 1992, pp.58-59.

McAleer, Neil. "On Creativity." *Omni,* 1989, pp. 42-102.

McMullin, David. "Lockerbie Insurance," *Scientific American,* January, 2002, pp. 15-16.

McNulty, Kevin T. "Fostering the Student-Centered Classroom Online," *T.H.E. Journal,* February, 2002, pp. 16-22.

Mednick, S. A. "The Associative Basis of the Creative Process." *Psychological Review*, 69, 1962, pp. 220-232.

Melcher, Richard A. and Michele Galen. "Milwaukee's Lesson Plan," *Business Week,* April 17, 1995, pp. 70-74.

Michalko, Michael, *Cracking Creativity.* Berkeley: Ten Speed Press. 1998.

Miller, William C. "Letters to the Editor: How To Kill Creativity", by Teresa M. Amabile, *Harvard Business Review,* November-December, 1998, p. 168.

Miller, Rockley L. "Learning Benefits of Interactive Technologies," *The Videodisc Monitor,* February 1990, pp. 15-17.

Mills, Kay. "British Columbia's Boom in Distance Education." *Crosstalk,* Fall, 2001, pp. 3-7.

Mirsky, Steve. "A Host with Infectious Ideas," *Scientific American*, May, 2001, pp. 32-33.

Morris, Mark reported by Diane L. Coutu. "Genius at Work," *Harvard Business Review,* October, 2001, pp. 63-68.

Moser-Wellerman, Annette. *Five Faces of Genius*, Viking Penguin Press, 2000.

Murray, Charles. J. *The Superman: the Story of Seymour Cray and the Technical Wizards Behind the Supercomputer*, New York: John Wiley. 1997.

Nadler, Gerald, Shozo Hibino with John Farrell. *Creative Solution Finding*. Rocklin, CA: Prima Publishing. 1995.

Nash, J. Madeleine. "Fertile Minds," *Time,* February 3, 1997, pp. 48-56.

Nash, J. Madeleine. "The Personality Genes," *Time,* April 27, 1998, pp. 60-61.

Nash, J. Madeleine, Alice Park and James Willwerth."Glimpses of the Mind," *Time,* July 17, 1995, pp. 44-52.

Neff, Wesley W. "Innovation and Discipline: An Interview with Bob Hebold," *The Leigh Advisor,* Summer, 2002, pp. 12-15.

Nickerson, Raymond S. *Dimensions of Thinking: A Critique*. In B. F. Jones & L. Idol (Eds.), *Dimensions of Thinking and Cognitive Instruction: Implications for Educational Reform,* Hillsdale, NJ., Vol.1,1990, pp. 495-509.

Nickerson, Raymond S. *Enhancing Creativity,* in R. J. Sternberg (Ed.), Handbook of Creativity, 1999, Cambridge: Cambridge University Press, pp. 392-430.

Nocera, Joseph. "Bill Gross Blew Through $800 Million in 8 Months (And He's Got Nothing to Show For it). Why is He Still Smiling?" *Fortune,* March 5, 2001, pp. 71-82.

"Nothing but Homework." *Forbes ASAP,* February 22, 1999, pp. 31-36.

Nylund, Andrea L. Learning Portal Opens to Authors, *Knowledge Management,* February, 2000, pp. 76.

Oelrich, Keith. "Virtual Schools: A 21 st. Century Strategy for Teacher Professional Development," *T.H.E. Journal,* June, 2001, pp. 48-50.

Oldham, Greg R. and Anne Cummings. "Employee Creativity: Personal and Contextual Factors at Work." *Academy of Management Journal,* Vol. 39, No. 3 1996, pp. 607-634.

Oliver, Myrna. "Michael Ritchie; Cost-Conscious Director," *L.A. Times*, April, 19, 2001, p. B8.

Paik, Han S. "One Intelligence or Many? Alternative Approaches to Cognitive Abilities," *Washington University,* August, 1998, pp. 1-5.

Pearl, Judea, "Reasoning with Belief Functions: An Analysis of Compatibility." *International Journal of Approximate Reasoning,* October 13, 1990, pp. 363-389.

Pellet, Jennifer. "Capturing the Innovation Premium," *CEO Magazine*, June, 2002, pp. 56-63.

Pennar, Karen. "How Many Smarts Do You Have?" *Business Week,* September 16, 1996, pp. 104-108.

Penrose, Roger. *The Emperor's New Mind*, New York: Oxford University Press, 1989, pp. 418.

Perkins, D. N. *Creativity and the Quest for Mechanism.* In R. J. Sternberg & E. F. Smith (Eds.), *The Psychology of Thought*, Cambridge: Cambridge University Press. 1988, pp. 309-336.

Piirto, Jane. *Understanding Those Who Create*, Gifted Psychology Press, Inc., Scottsdale: Arizona, 1998.

Pinker, S. *Language Learnability and Language Development*, Cambridge, Mass: Harvard University Press, 1984.

Plato, *The Last Days of Socrates*, Edited by Hugh Tredennick. Penguin, 1951.

Plomin, Robert & John L. DeFries. Scientific American, May, 1998, pp.62-69.

Policastro, Emma and Howard Gardner. *From Case Studies to Robust Generalizations: An Approach to the Study of Creativity. In* Sternberg, Robert J., (Ed.) *Handbook of Creativity.* Cambridge: Cambridge University Press, 1999, pp. 213-225.

Port, Otis. "Why Johnny May Learn to Add," *Business Week,* December 13, 1999, pp. 108-114.

Psychology 499. "Students Apply Theory to the Real World," *University of Southern California Chronicle,* April 12, 1999, pp. 1, 6.

Quinn, James Brian, Philip Anderson and Sydney Finkelstein. "Leveraging Intellect," *Academy of Management Executive*, Vol. 10, No. 3, 1996, pp.7-27.

Quirden, Anna. "A Good Girl, a Great Woman," *Newsweek,* July 30, 2001, pp. 59-64.

Raeb Paul. "The Brain's Many Mansions," *Business Week*, December 20, 1999, pp. 36.

Ratnesar, Romesh. "The Bite on Teachers," *Time,* July 20,1998, pp. 22-25.

Renzulli, J. S. The Three-Ring Conception of Giftedness: A Developmental Model.

Restak, Richard M., Brainscapes. New York: *Hyperion.* 1995. (1986).

Robinson, Ken. *Out of Our Minds,* Oxford: Capstone Publishing Limited, 2001.

Roe, A. *Psychological Approaches to Creativity in Science. In* A. Rothenberg & C.R. Hausman (Eds.), *The Creativity Question*, Durham, NC: Duke University Press, 1976. pp. 165-175. (Reprinted from M. A. Coler & H. K. Hughes, Eds. *Essays on Creativity in the Sciences*, New York: New York University Press. 1976. pp.152-154, 166-172, 177-182.)

Ross, Steven, "Rethinking Thinking." *Modern Management*, (Feb-Mar, 1990), 52-58.

Rowe, Alan J. and Boulgardies, James. *Managerial Decision Making*. Englewood Cliffs N.J.: Prentice-Hall, 1992.

Rowe, Alan J. and Fred Bahr, "An Heuristic Approach to Managerial Problem Solving," *Journal of Economics and Business*, 1973, pp. 159-161.

Rowe, Alan J. and Mason, Richard. *Managing with Style*. San Francisco: Jossey-Bass Publishers, 1987.

Rowe, Alan J. *The Meta Logic of Cognitively Based Heuristics*, In Watkins, P.R., and Eliot, L.B., *Expert Systems in Business and Finance*, New York: John Wiley, 1993, pp. 109-127.

Rowe, Alan J., Richard Mason and Bruce Katz. "Are You in the Right Job?" *Newsweek, Management Digest*, Fall 1988, Vol. 1, Issue 3.

Schooler, J. W., & Melcher, J. *The Ineffability of Insight. In* S. M. Smith, T. B. Ward, & R. A. Finke (Eds.), *The Creative Cognition Approach*. Cambridge, MA: MIT Press. 1995, pp. 97-133.

Seligman, Dan. "College: A Reality Check," *Forbes,* July 27, 1998, pp. 73-75.

Shalley, Christina E., Lucly L. Gilson, and Terry C. Blum. "Matching Creativity Requirements and the Work Environment: Effects on Satisfaction and Intentions to Leave." *Academy of Management Journal*, Vol. 43, No.2, 2000. pp. 215-223.

Shea, Rachel Hartigan and Ulrich Boser. "So Where's the Beef?" *U.S. News & World Report,* October 15, 2001, pp. 44 -54.

Shouksmith, G. *Intelligence, Creativity and Cognitive Style*. London.

Shrivastava, Paul. Book Reviews: "Mindscapes in Management," by Magoroh Maruyama, *Academy of Management Review,* Vol. 21, No. 2, 1996, pp. 558-579.

Simon, Herbert A. *Administrative Behavior,* Simon and Schuster Adult Publishing Group, 1997.

Simonton, D. K. *Greatness: Who Makes History and Why?* New York: Guilford. 1994.

Skrzycki, Cindy, et al, "Risk Takers," *U.S. News & World Report*, Jan. 26, 1987, pp. 60-67.

Smith, Gerald, and Jerry Debenham. "Automating University Teaching by the Year 2000." *T.H.E. Journal,* August, 1993, pp. 71-75.

Smith, I. L. "IQ, Creativity, and the Taxonomy of Educational Objectives: Cognitive Domain." *Journal of Experimental Education*, 38(4), 1970, pp. 58-60.

Smith, I. L. "IQ, Creativity and Achievement: Interaction and Threshold," *Multivariate Behavioral Research*, 6(1), 1971, pp. 51-62.

Smith, S. M., Ward, T. B., & Finke, R. A. (Eds.) *The Creative Cognition Approach,* Cambridge, MA: MIT Press, 1995.

Snyder, Benson R. "Literacy and Numeracy: Two Ways of Knowing," *Daedalus*, *Journal of the American Academy of Arts and Sciences*, Spring, 1990, pp. 233, 237.

Steen, Margaret. "Learning is No Longer a Luxury." *Infoworld,* September 20, 1999, pp. 77-78.

Stein, Lynn Andrea. "Science and Engineering in Knowledge Representation and Reasoning," *AI Magazine,* Winter, 1996, pp. 77-83.

Stepanek, Marcia. "You Have Nothing To Lose But Your Cubicle." *Business Week* October 16, 2000, P. 26.

Sternberg, *Handbook of Creativity,* (1991, Ch. 14).

Sternberg, R. J. "Implicit Theories of Intelligence, Creativity, and Wisdom," *Journal of Personality and Social Psychology. (4) 9, 1985,* pp. 607-627.

Sternberg, R. J., and Lubart, T. I. *Defying the Crowd: Cultivating Creativity in a Culture of Conformity.* New York: Free Press. 1995.

Sternberg, R. J. *Beyond IQ: A Triarchic Theory of Human Intelligence*. Cambridge.

Sternberg, Robert J. (Ed.) *Handbook of Creativity.* Cambridge: Cambridge University Press, 1999.

Stewart, Thomas A. "Brain Power." *Fortune,* March 17, 1997, pp. 105-110.

Stroud, Ruth. "Learning from Afar," *Los Angeles Times,* January 14, 2002, p. U4.

Sturm, Paul. "Artificial Intelligence," *Smart Money*, August, 2002, pp. 48-49.

Sutliff, Usha. "New Tools Bring Math Instruction Into the 21st Century." *University of Southern California Chronicle*, February 4, 2002, p. 4.

Sutton, Robert I. "The Weird Rules of Creativity." *Harvard Business Review*, September, 2001, pp. 94-103.

Symonds, William C., with Ann Theresa Palmer and Hillary Hylton. "How to Fix America's Schools," *Business Week*, March, 19, 2001, pp. 67-80.

"Mind Mapping: A New Way to Think on Paper." *Fortune*, Nov. 16, 1992, p. 12.

Taft, Martin. *Learning Applied to an Engineering Education*, Doctoral Dissertation, USC. 1966.

"Teach, Don't Train." *The Economist*, March 31,1990, pp. 17-18.

"The Creators." *Modern Maturity*, March-April, 2000, pp. 37-43.

"The Innovation Mandate." *Chief Executive*, June 1998. pp. 52-64.

"The Innovative Enterprise." *Harvard Business Review*, August 2002, p. 6.

"The State of Innovation." *Technology Review*, June, 2002, pp. 55-63.

Thompson, Tom. "The Elements of Design," *Byte*, August, 1996, pp. 1-8.

Toch, Thomas, "The New Education Bazaar." *U.S. News & World Report*, April 27,1998, pp. 34-46.

Tolson, Jay, "E=mcΣ Got That? Sure?" *U.S. News & World Report*. December 18, 2000, pp. 54-55.

Torrance, E. P., *Creativity Research in Education: Still Alive*. In I. A. Taylor & J. W. Getzels (Eds.), Perspectives in Creativity Chicago: Aldine, 1975, 278-296.

Torrance, E. P., *Explorations in Creative Thinking in the Early School Years: A Progress Report. In* C. W. Taylor & F. Barron (Eds.), *Scientific Creativity: Its Recognition and Development.* Wiley: New York, 1963. 173-183.

Verity, John W. "Umpteen Gigabytes of Genius." *Business Week,* February 17, 1997, p. 15.

Von Hipple, Eric, Stefan Tomke and Mary Sonnac. "Creating Breakthroughs at 3M," *Harvard Business Review,* Sept.- Oct. 1999, pp. 47-57.

Wagner, Betsy. "The Ninth Grader Who Answered Euclid," *U.S. News & World Report,* December 23, 1996, p. 20.

Wallace, D., and Gruber, H. *Creative People at Work.* New York: Oxford University Press, 1990.

Wallace, James. *Bill Gates and the Making of the Microsoft Empire,* Harper Collins, 1999.

Wallach, M., & Kogan. *"N' Modes of Thinking in Young Children,* New York: Holt, Rinehart, & Winston, 1965.

Ward, T. B., & Sifonis, C. M. "Task Demands and Generative Thinking: What Changes and What Remains the Same?" *Journal of Creative Behavior,* 31, 1997, pp. 245-259.

Ward, T. B., Finke, R. A., & Smith, S. M. *Creativity and the Mind: Discovering the Genius Within.* New York: Plenum Press. 1995. pp.8-9, 49-50, 51-52, 87-88, 115.

Ward, T. B., Smith, S. M., and Vaid, J. "Conceptual Structures and Processes in Creative Thought," *In* T. B. Ward, S. M. Smith, & J. Vaid (Eds.), "Creative Thought: An Investigation of Conceptual Structures and Processes," Washington, DC: *American Psychological Association,* 1997, pp. 1-27.

Ward, T. B. *What's Old About New Ideas?* in S. M. Smith, T. B. Ward, & R. A. Finke (Eds.) The Creative Cognition Approach , Cambridge, MA: MIT Press, 1995, pp. 157-179.

Webb, Michael. "Creativity Unbound," *UCLA Magazine,* Spring, 1999, p. 32.

Wetlaufer, Suzy. "What's Stifling the Creativity at CoolBurst?" *Harvard Business Review* September-October, 1997, pp. 36-51.

Whitaker, George W. "First-Hand Observations on Tele-Course Teaching," *T.H.E. Journal,* August, 1995, pp. 65-68.

Wilgoren, Jodi. "Jacob Getzels, 89, Educator and Researcher on Creativity." *L.A. Times,* April, 2001.

Wolpert, John D. "Breaking Out of the Innovation Box," *Harvard Business Review* August, 2002, pp. 77-83.

Wright, Karen. "How Do Cognitive Abilities Relate to General Intelligence?" *Scientific American,* May, 1998, p. 64., September, 2000, pp. 148-154.

Zalewski, Daniel. "Eureka It Ain't," *Fortune,* June 10, 1996, pp. 141-142.

Zeki, Semir. *Inner Vision: An Exploration of Art and the Brain.* Oxford: Oxford University Press. 1999.

Zorpette, Glenn. "The Asian Paradox: Huge Classes, High Scores." *Scientific American,* November, 2001, p. 84.

Zuckerman, Mortimer, B. "The Times of Our Lives," *US News and World Report,* Dec. 27, 1999, pp. 68-69.

INDEX

Printing press, 10
Problem-solving, creative, 67–68
    defining the problems, 70
    example, 70–72
    finding solutions, 69–70
Prusiner, Stanley, 54
Purchasing agents, and personal
    preference in solution, 81

Q

Quanta, 137
Quantum cryptography, 138
Quantum leap, need for, 122
Quantum theory, 137

R

Rand Corporation, 133
Rationality, 81
Reasoning, 32
    and creative problem-solving, 73–74
Recognition, and creative individuals,
    133–134
Reinforcement, 96
Rembrandt van Rijn, 55, 62–63
Remote surgery, 79
Rigid approaches to problem solving, 72
Risk taking, 68
Roadblocks to perception, 31
Robinson, Kathryn, 105
Robinson, Ken, 90–91
Robotics, 138
Roosevelt, Eleanor, 56
Roosevelt, Franklin D., 66
Rosen, Ben, 134–135
Rudimentary calendars, and early
    ancestors, 10
Rutan, Burt, 131
Rutherford, Lord, 32

S

Saint-Saëns, 106
Salk, Jonas, 57, 66, 83
Sample, Stephen, 118

Sand, George, 16–17
SAP, 137
Schlesinger, Arthur Jr., 2
Schweitzer, Albert, 57
Scientists, and observation and research,
    21
Senior managers, creative styles of, 121
Sequential model of instruction, 104–105
Shakespeare, William, 57, 63–64
Sharpless, Barry, 54
Shaw, Gordon, 106
Shockley, William, 30
Silicon wafer, 139
Simonton, Dean Keith, 58
Sisson, Richard, 100
Skinner, B. F., 30
Smart cards, 137
Snowflake Model of Creativity, 23
Society, and creative people, 14
Socrates, 14, 93
Solberg, Peer, 82
Southern California Gas, 78
Specialized training, 48
Speed of light, 22
Stanford Center for Professional
    Development (SCPD), 110
Starkweather, Gary, 130–132
Steinbeck, John, 54
Sternberg, Robert, 9
Stradivarius, Antonio, 18, 56, 65
Stravinsky, Igor Fyodorovich, 55, 65
Structure, finding a balance between
    freedom and, 50
Student differences, 102–103
Sutton, Robert, 130–132
Synectics, 32
Synthetic antibodies, 136

T

Taft, Martin, 96
Teaching process, automation of, 111
Teamwork, 127
Technology:
    and education, 111–113